Fast

Wor

Fast Lives

Women Who Use

Crack Cocaine

Claire E. Sterk

Temple University Press   PHILADELPHIA

Temple University Press, Philadelphia 19122
Copyright © 1999 by Temple University
All rights reserved
Published 1999
Printed in the United States of America

⊗ The paper used in this publication meets the requirements of
American National Standard for Information Sciences—Permanence
of Paper for Printed Library Materials, ANSI Z39.48-1984

Library of Congress Cataloging-in-Publication Data

Sterk, Claire E., 1957–
    Fast lives : women who use crack cocaine / Claire E. Sterk.
        p.   cm.
    Includes bibliographical references and index.
    ISBN 1-56639-671-9 (cloth : alk. paper). — ISBN 1-56639-672-7
(pbk. : alk. paper)
    1. Women—Drug use—United States.   2. Crack (Drug)—United
States.   3. Women—United States—Social conditions.   I. Title.
HV5824.W6S8   1999
362.29'82'0820973—dc21   98-35779
                                                                    CIP

Contents

Acknowledgments

This book would not have been possible without the help of many people. In college and graduate school, I was very fortunate to learn about ethnographic research from Frank Bovenkerk, Institute of Criminology, University of Utrecht, and Charles Kaplan, University of Limburg. My first job as a drug researcher was with Charlie at Erasmus University in Rotterdam. In the United States, I benefited enormously from the support of Bill Kornblum, Terry Williams, Charles Winick, the late Vernon Boggs, and others of the Graduate School and University Center, City University of New York. They always were available to listen to my stories, to coach me, and to provide emotional support. Bill and his family treated me as a member. Vernon was my "partner in crime." He was a true friend, always there to watch my back. Most importantly, he taught me to believe in myself.

The National Institute on Drug Abuse (NIDA) provided a substantial portion of the funding for this research (R29DA-07407; RO1DA09819; RO1DA10642). Many staff members made the research possible, and special mention should be made of my project officers, Mario DeLaRosa, Coryl Jones, Susan Coyle, Helen Cesari, Elizabeth Lambert, and Rich Needle. The Neighborhood Research Program of the Foundation for Child Development in New York supported research on the impact of community characteristics on the lives of young children. In addition, a grant from the Research Office of Georgia State University allowed me to expand the breadth of my work. Despite the various funding sources, the research became known as project FAST, the Female Atlanta Study. Many of the women in this study referred to the fast lifestyle associated with crack cocaine use, which gave added meaning to the project's name.

Many colleagues and friends have provided feedback on my ideas at professional meetings or during informal interactions. Among them, I especially would like to thank Mike Agar, the late Patrick Biernacki, Myra Burnett, Eloise Dunlap, Sam Friedman, Don DesJarlais, Billy DiFazio, Michael Giles, Laetitia Goldstein, Jim Hall, John Hagendorn, Nic Kozel, Selma Marks, Rani Marx, Jeanne McGettigan, Art Murphy, Sheigla Murphy, Al Pach, David Petersen, Richard Rothenberg, Chuck Rutheiser, Marcel Scholtes, the late John Waters, Wayne Wiebel, and Terry Williams. They all contributed to the content of the book or to my mental well-being. Patsy Ulmer's phone calls and the many relaxing hours with Carol Hansen boosted my spirits.

Countless people assisted with the completion of this project. I fear I will forget to mention someone and I ask their forgiveness in advance. I would like to thank Wanda Baker, Susan Maleski, and Tanya Sharpe, who participated in the early days of the research. In addition, the following individuals contributed with interviewing, mapping, transcribing, and many other tasks: Lotta Danielson, Kathy Dolan, Lithia Givens, Susan Hart, Stephani Hatch, Sarah Heathcote, Shirley Jordan, Lee Jenkins, Cecilia Lyles, Yvonne "Kiki" Medina, and the late Sterling White. Many other community members and graduate students helped with the research, a process described by many as having opened their eyes to lives different from their own. They kept their good humor even when life got hectic. Rhonda Mullen always took time to edit my work in progress, and she must have had some good laughs as she polished my early drafts. I aspire to become a writer like her. Michael Ames of Temple University Press provided the final push to complete this project and I thank him for his assistance.

During my earlier years as a child in a coal mining town in the Netherlands, I learned about the relativity of life, its joys and its struggles. At high school, I learned about drugs and their negative consequences. I watched friends getting sick and losing control. My parents, Sjef and Thea Sterk, allowed me to become the person I am. They often wondered where I was headed. My siblings Liset and John and their families never tired of hearing another story.

Sometimes I wonder how the world around me continued to function. My "special" daughters, Kristin and Shelley constantly reminded me of the joys of life. They were perfect adolescents and have matured into wonderful young adults. While they requested regular updates on my progress, they also made sure I found time to play with them and give back rubs. Kirk Elifson, my husband, never complained about "having to do it all." His contributions would be too great to list here, but he'll always be my "kabouter." I know I pushed limits, caused him to be concerned about my safety, and, at times, was obsessed with the FAST women. I thank him for accepting all my flaws and I dedicate this book to him.

My greatest debt is to the women whose stories appear in the following pages. They must remain anonymous. I hope the reader senses their strength. Already vulnerable, they were willing to talk openly about their lives. I will never be able to truly express my gratitude to them. They were willing to let me, a stranger, into their lives. This work has allowed me to develop close friendships with women whom I otherwise might never have met.

Fast Lives

Women Who Use Crack Cocaine

Introduction

Alice, a slender, thirty-two-year-old African American woman, was very content with her life until she started using drugs. She was sixteen at the time. When I met her, she was in her late twenties and an injection drug user. By then, she also had an eleven-year-old son and a two-year-old daughter. Her older sister was taking care of the children to allow Alice to focus on some changes she wanted to make in her life. Her biggest goal was to become free from drug addiction. Although she had been in drug treatment three times in the past several years, each time she was caught with "dirty urine."

Alice grew up in the Deep South and spent many childhood summers at her grandmother's house in rural Georgia. Her mother, her two older sisters, and her baby brother preferred to stay in the city. She lovingly retold some of her grandmother's stories, stories about bygone times, about her mama as a little girl, and even, sometimes, frightening tales of ghosts who resided in the house.

Shortly after her sixteenth birthday, Alice learned that her best girlfriend, LaDonna, had been caught with marijuana and sent away to live with relatives in Mississippi. The two teens never saw each other again, and Alice often wondered about LaDonna's life. Alice missed her friend. They had never really talked about drugs, beyond agreeing that they didn't like the kids at school who used them. After LaDonna tried marijuana, Alice found herself curious. The kids she had avoided in the past became her marijuana suppliers. They teased her for having been a little sweetheart for so long.

During her senior year in high school, Alice stole money from her mother's purse, an event that marked the beginning of a chaotic life. Her mother, seeing Alice headed for trouble, broke down and sought

1

the advice of a white woman for whom she worked. This woman and her family provided the only contacts Alice had with whites while she was growing up. But Alice was furious. She felt betrayed by her own mother.

She thought a lot about running away from home, but instead she often stayed over at friends' places or slept outside when the weather was nice. She came and went at will. Her sisters began to distance themselves from her, treating her as if she was no longer one of them. Shortly before she turned eighteen, Alice fell in love with Bill and soon moved in with him. She knew that Bill used heroin. Through him, she developed contacts with other drug users. At first she didn't use heroin, initially because she had no interest and later because she was pregnant with their son. On the boy's first birthday, Alice persuaded Bill to give her some heroin. Within six months, he was injecting her with heroin several times a week.

Three years into the relationship, Bill was arrested, and Alice was left behind to struggle with her withdrawal from heroin. One of Bill's female acquaintances injected her a few times and then finally taught Alice how to inject herself. For a while, Alice supported her habit by injecting other new users who were afraid to inject themselves or who did not know how to do it.

Slightly more than two years before this study was done, Alice and the father of her second child began experimenting with crack cocaine. She described her crack cocaine use as more addictive and expensive than the heroin habit. She began working as a prostitute to pay for her own and her partner's drugs. Soon afterwards, she discovered that she was pregnant. The father left, and a week later she miscarried.

One of Alice's dreams is to live with a nice man who loves and cares about her. She sees herself living in a big house with a two-car garage, and, of course, she is drug free. In the meantime, however, she is struggling to survive from day to day. The last time I spoke with Alice, she was worried about AIDS. She had been losing weight and had learned that a man with whom she had had sex and injected drugs several *years before had died of AIDS. We talked about the advantages and disadvantages of HIV testing. When I dropped her off at home, she joked about how she had gotten mad at her mother for seeking guidance from the white family for whom she worked. Now Alice herself was asking advice from a white person, though she pointed out that I wasn't "white," but Dutch. Somehow this distinction made it easier for her to accept me.*

Alice's experiences resemble those of many of the other women in project FAST, the Female Atlanta Study. Their stories are similar to each other in many ways but different in others. Curiosity and peer pressure led many of these women to experiment with drugs. Others were introduced to drugs by friends, often their boyfriends.

Most women in project FAST tried other drugs before they used crack cocaine. Prostitution frequently was the means through which they supported their crack cocaine habit, but many women also paid for their drugs by participating in the drug business or through "hustles" such as shoplifting, credit card fraud, and thefts from motor vehicles.

One of the shared aspects of these women's lives was their stigmatization as drug users. They were all too familiar with many of the prevailing negative images of crack cocaine users. They had heard them over and over—from judges, from correction officers, and sometimes from their best friends and relatives. These people depicted them as irresponsible, uncaring, and unreliable. They have called them "crack whores," "crack freaks," "chicken heads," and worse, all terms used to describe women who exchange sex for crack cocaine, a phenomenon commonly associated with female crack use.[1]

Women who use crack cocaine meet with harsher disapproval from society than their male counterparts seem to do. This tendency may in part be due to the societal denial of illicit drug use among women in general. Even prior to the mid-1980s, when crack cocaine began dominating the U.S. street drug market, the extent of female drug use was often downplayed because it undermined society's expectations of women. Being a drug user and a woman are generally seen as incompatible social roles. In a study of women who use heroin, for example, Marsha Rosenbaum (1981) described how their options decreased as drug use became more central in their lives.

Previous studies of female drug users, including crack cocaine users, have often focused on these women's reproductive responsibilities, especially the impact of their drug use on the development of the unborn fetus or on their role as mothers (Chasnoff, 1989; Chavkin, 1990; Kearney, Murphy, and Rosenbaum, 1994; Lieb and Sterk-Elifson, 1995). Other researchers have explored the ways in which women support their drug habit, identifying prostitution as a common means of support (Goldstein, 1979; Inciardi, Lockwood, Pottieger, 1993; Ratner, 1993). Only recently have researchers linked the involvement of female crack cocaine users to illicit activities other than prostitution (Dunlap, Johnson, and Manwar, 1994; Fagan 1994).

This study approaches crack cocaine habits and their consequences from the point of view of the female users. It is a study of women who are active crack cocaine users and who are not in drug treatment, prison, or any other institutional setting. The women's accounts, as presented in their own words throughout the text, frequently refer to their failures and despair as well as their successes and hopes. The women in project FAST often gave contradictory explanations for their situations. Their stories expressed passion and motivation but also apathy and manipulation. On one hand, they blamed society for oversimplifying their problems, for ignoring the causes of their drug use, for offering only piecemeal solutions. On the other hand, they acknowledged their personal responsibilities, their mistakes, and their own weaknesses.

Even though they did not anticipate the long-term impact of drug use on their lives, they acknowledged having at least some prior understanding of the possible negative consequences. When they first confronted problems that arose as a consequence of their drug intake, they never entertained the option of stopping their use. While some women, like Alice, sought assistance to reduce or cease their drug use, they often were unable to do so. Initially, Alice tried to convince me that her failure to quit using drugs was due to the attitude of the drug treatment staff. When I challenged her, she burst into a rage. The following field notes capture the essence of this encounter:

> Alice got really mad. I guess I was only supposed to listen. I did tell her that I wanted to hear her story, but I couldn't let her get away with this. What got to her most was when I told her I did not believe that it was the staff's fault. She didn't understand why I just wouldn't believe that the treatment staff intentionally put drugs in her urine. She pulled the insider-outsider game. I never would be able to understand her because only addicts could understand addicts. She called me racist. I felt hurt, and I became angry as well. Suddenly, Alice's mood shifted, and she began seeking my pity. She almost convinced me that I could not understand her. Tired and weary, we agreed that society was screwed up. There wasn't much we could do about that. She could, however, change her way of life and try again to become drug free.

Throughout this research, I never doubted that I wanted to become involved with the women, that I wanted to gain a better understanding of their lives. Frequently, I grappled with the tension between my desire to make a difference in their situation and the realization that this would require tackling larger social forces such as racism and poverty. As I hope this book will show, the lives of these women exemplified the interconnectedness of gender, class, and race (hooks, 1991; Andersen and Collins, 1992). Most of the women in project FAST were African American and were raised in impoverished families. The Hispanic women in the study also alluded to racism and poverty, and many of the white women referred to discrimination against "white trash."

Several women in project FAST believed that "getting off drugs" might enhance their quality of life but would not necessarily provide them with adequate housing, educational opportunities, or better jobs. Those women often used such reasoning to rationalize their continued drug use.

Methodology

One of the main goals of this study was to develop a clearer understanding of the lives of female crack cocaine users. During a four-year period, information was collected in Atlanta, Georgia, by engaging in hundreds of hours of participant observation, holding countless informal conversations, leading group discussions and focus groups, and conducting in-depth interviews with 149 women who were active users of crack cocaine. As is typical of qualitative research, I supplemented the *a priori* research topics with others identified as relevant by the study participants themselves. The initial, limited list of study topics focused on general descriptions of an average day in the women's lives, their significant relationships and roles, and their future expectations. It soon grew to include issues such as drug treatment, violence, and HIV/AIDS.

In these pages, the reader will not find epidemiological statements about the prevalence and incidence of crack cocaine use, the statistical association between crack cocaine use and crime or HIV infection, or predictors of drug use. Instead, the reader will hear fragments of the stories the women in this study told about their lives.[2] I have supplemented these stories with data collected through informal conversations, group discussions, and my own observations. Critics may dismiss this information as anecdotal and unscientific. However, by modifying the original research questions and allowing new topics to emerge, it became possible to gather information relevant to crack cocaine use that otherwise might have gone undiscovered.

One of the first steps in the study involved ethnographic mapping to identify geographical areas where female crack cocaine users could be found. The selection process included a compilation of available information from formal sources such as local law enforcement officials, drug treatment staff, emergency department personnel, and other social and health service providers. Informal sources—taxi drivers, merchants, members of community organizations, and drug users—provided additional guidance. Upon selection of the study neighborhoods, community consultants were hired as project staff. These consultants were women from the area who served as liaisons between the community and the researchers. Early on they stressed the importance of naming the research project. They wanted a name that clearly emphasized that this study was about women only, but also one that would not stress the study's focus on drug use. After much debate, we chose project FAST, the Female Atlanta STudy.

One of the initial research steps in the ethnographic mapping included observing the physical and social infrastructures of the study neighborhoods. Findings from these observations were recorded in specific memo logs, which also made reference to information gathered during any informal conversations that occurred during the observation times. Initially, these conversations tended to be limited to chats about the weather, someone's garden or car, or other superficial topics. Soon, however, a number of residents asked for more information about the research goals and objectives and began questioning my interest in the neighborhood. These exchanges offered the opportunity to introduce the study and to begin asking residents their opinions about specific issues such as the prevalence of drugs in their neighborhood and their impact on their community. Some residents worried that the research might give their neighborhood a bad reputation as a drug-infested area. One of the main contributions of the community consultants was that they facilitated entrée into the neighborhoods. Not only were they known to many of the residents but they were also familiar with the local power structure. For example, depending on the community, information sessions were set up with local church leaders, members of the board of tenant associations, store owners, or landlords. Some leaders and residents were unsettled by the presence of a white woman who spoke with a foreign accent. Gaining trust took time, and some individuals continued to have reservations. The following field notes reveal some of the trust dynamics.

> During the meeting with Ms. Ranton, the tenants' association president, she never made eye contact with me. She did not use my name and referred to me as "her." The one time I tried to say something, she totally ignored me. She told Tony, the

community consultant, that she would not hold her personally responsible if it didn't work out. . . . The neighborhood barbeque and health fair were very well attended. Ms. Ranton came by, but we never got beyond the "how are you doing?" stage. She walked up to me while we were cleaning up and commented, "I sure am glad to see that you are doing something for the neighborhood. The people here need more." She wanted us to organize a clothing fair for the upcoming winter. I told her I would check into it, which resulted in a sarcastic remark from her about knowing what that meant. I guess she interpreted my response as a polite no, as a cop out. . . . We held the clothing fair. Ms. Ranton mentioned to Tony that we at least came through. We now may put up posters and distribute flyers.

Participant observation—the observation of human behavior and actions—was a major component of the ethnographic mapping (Becker, 1963; Adler, 1985). These observations involved "hanging out," developing initial contacts and trust, and continuously checking and rechecking information and our interpretations of it. The participant observation sessions posed many challenges. Obviously, "hanging out" in a public setting was less difficult than spending time in a semi-public or private crack house where people were getting high, exchanging sex for drugs, or reminiscing about criminal activities. Typically, as my knowledge and understanding increased, the observations became more focused. Being the only white person involved in the participant observation, my experiences sometimes differed from those of the community consultants who assisted with many of the sessions and who, with the exception of one Hispanic woman, were all African American. These field notes address part of the negotiation of my role:

Finally some of the people nod their head when they see me. The guys on the corner even asked me how I was doing. Linda, a woman whom I knew from my earlier research in the area, had told them that I was okay. Instead of asking me, one of the guys asked her what kind of business I was into. She told them I was a professor, a professor of the streets. I had told her of my earlier experience of being asked by a drug dealer where I had bought my university ID. She told them about this. One of the guys tried to convince me that he knew everything that was going on in the neighborhood. He also asked me for condoms. I had been hanging out with some of the AIDS outreach workers, who visit the community every other week and who hand out HIV risk-reduction materials, including condoms. Especially the condoms made me popular. I began carrying some all the time. I also seem to have become a major supplier of cigarettes, rides, and meals. The one thing I refused to give people was money. Linda thought it was good for me to listen to their bullshit. Her main message to me is to be myself, and I'll be treated like everyone else. When I asked her what that meant, she responded, "They'll love you, and they'll use you."

A crack house manager in one of the neighborhoods stressed the importance of "following your own gut feeling, just like the rest of us." This often meant leaving the setting when tensions arose or when ongoing activities became too stressful to watch.[3] Philippe Bourgois (1995) described some of the violence and abuse he encountered during his participant observation research in Spanish Harlem, New York. Patricia Adler (1985) admitted feeling threatened at times during her study of drug dealers. While I never directly witnessed abuse and violence, I did see the results of it and often felt frustrated because there was little I could do to prevent it from happening again.

In addition to guiding the selection of the study neighborhoods, the ethnographic mapping helped reach a wide cross-section of female crack cocaine users who might be interested in participating in the study. Initially, the selection of study participants focused on women who were eighteen or older, who used crack cocaine, and who lived in the study neighborhoods. It soon became clear, however, that additional criteria such as the length of drug use, the means of supporting the drug habit, the introduction to drug use, and the motherhood status of most women were distinguishing aspects of their lives.

I learned that some women had used other drugs, such as marijuana and heroin, in the past, while crack cocaine was the first illicit drug for others. Still other women used crack cocaine in combination with drugs such as marijuana or heroin. This increased knowledge of the women's drug-use patterns resulted in a more specific recruitment process, also referred to as theoretical sampling. This sampling spawned the organization of chapter 2 around the women's patterns of income generation and the social context in which crack cocaine use occurred. Some women mainly supported their crack cocaine use through their involvement in the drug business. They became known, for purposes of this study, as the Queens of the Scene, a term they suggested themselves. Others had a history of criminal involvement and maintained their crack cocaine habit largely through earnings from their illicit activities. This group, the Hustlers, tended not to engage in prostitution, a support strategy common among a third group that I termed the Hookers. Finally there were the Older Struggling Rookies, who began using crack cocaine when they were in their thirties or older and often lacked purchasing power, which forced them to barter sex for crack cocaine.

Researchers frequently base their decisions about how many and what type of people they want to include in their sample on available statistics. Because the statistics on female drug use are limited, it is more difficult to decide how many and what type of women to include. A practice generally followed in ethnographic research is to continue to collect data until no new information is discovered. I used this strategy and recruited women until no new themes emerged, a point also referred to by qualitative researchers as saturation.

Those women who fit the study's eligibility criteria were invited for an individual in-depth interview and/or a focus group. If they decided to participate, the study was explained in detail and they had the opportunity to ask questions prior to signing a consent form.[4]

In-depth interviewing involves guided but open-ended conversations with study participants. The interviewer is required to be a careful listener who constantly integrates information and, where necessary, probes for elaboration. Sometimes this approach resulted in dialogues about topics that were unrelated to the study.

The interview guide for project FAST covered topics such as family background, relational history, mothering and parenting, drug-use history, drugs and sex, social support, and future expectations. As is typical of in-depth interviewing, the final content of the interviews depended partly on the relationship with the respondent. For example, it always seemed more difficult to challenge contradictions in the stories of those women who were emotionally upset and who began crying during the interview than it was with women who laughed and joked. Differences also depended on the extent to which the women felt comfortable talking about intimate subjects. While some women seemed to have no difficulty sharing their involvement in illegal activities, others understated or denied their participation in such hustles. Several times, women refused to admit that they participated in illegal activities until I pointed out the discrepancy between their reported income and their expenses. In response, some women shrugged their shoulders, while others opened up and revealed their sources of additional income.

The in-depth interviews were conducted at a variety of locations, including a centrally located downtown office, residences, hotels, fast-food restaurants, and my car. All formal, in-depth interviews were tape-recorded and transcribed, and they lasted between ninety minutes and four hours, with an average length of two hours.

Several focus groups were conducted with interviewees as well as with crack cocaine-using women who were not interviewed. The focus groups were used to make sure that the data were interpreted accurately. These groups also were helpful when the information from the participant observation differed from the interview information. There were crack house managers, for example, who denied allowing drug sales in spite of my observations to the contrary. The data were also compared on the individual level. A common scenario involved women who denied getting high in a crack house but were observed smoking in a crack house. This process of comparing the information from different data sources, also referred to as triangulation, increased the validity of the data.

The Women in Project FAST

The 149 women who participated in in-depth interviews for project FAST all fit the study eligibility criteria. They used crack cocaine. They were eighteen years of age or older. They lived in a study neighborhood. They were not in drug treatment or any other institutional setting. While each woman had her own story, many of the stories shared common elements.

The youngest woman enrolled in this study was eighteen years old, and the oldest participant was fifty-eight. The women's median age of thirty-three years may appear relatively old for crack cocaine users, but many of these women experimented with other drugs prior to making crack cocaine their drug of choice. According to the National Household Survey on Drug Abuse—one of the main sources of information on the prevalence of illegal drug use in the U.S. population—drug use tends to be associated with low levels of education. In this survey, individuals who dropped out of high school reported drug-use rates 2.5 times higher than those for college graduates (United States Department of Health and Human Services, 1995). Almost half of the women in project FAST failed to complete high school. They dropped out because of pregnancy, drug use, or parental pressure to find a job and contribute to the household income. Compared to the national statistics on drug use and education, a relatively large proportion of the women in this study completed high school. Among the high school graduates, one in five women attended college for one or more years, and six women received a college degree. The median educational attainment for the women in project FAST was twelve years.

With the exception of the Queens of the Scene, the women's median income was near or below the poverty level. Most women reported multiple sources of income, including illegal activities (70.5 percent), legal employment (28.7 percent), government subsidies (27.5 percent), financial support from relatives (28.7 percent), and other sources (15.1 percent). While slightly over one-fourth of the women received financial assistance from relatives, the amounts tended to be small and were contributed only during times of crisis. Almost half received all or nearly all of their living expenses from illegal activities.

Although some women were raised in middle-class families, their lives no longer reflected this social background at the time of the interview. Most of the women in project FAST were members of the underclass, a term commonly used among social scientists to refer to the poor. William Wilson, in his book, *The Truly Disadvantaged* (1987), used the term to refer to African Americans who faced poverty due to changes in the labor market, primarily the decrease of low-level, low-skilled jobs. Unfortunately, the term underclass has become a stereotype associated with racial minorities and the "undeserving poor." Among policy makers, it has become an excuse for failure to develop constructive policies. For example, recent discussions of welfare reform and a reduction in funding for anti-poverty programs are based on the assumption that all members of the underclass are unwilling to work. The stories of the women in project FAST revealed that the major use of their income from welfare was for basic necessities such as rent, food, and other elementary needs—not drugs. In addition, the women's welfare status motivated a number of them to attempt to control or limit their drug habit.

Slightly more than half of the women in project FAST were African American (53.7 percent), reflecting the ethnic composition of the city of Atlanta, in which two-thirds of the residents are African American (Atlanta Regional Commission, 1995). The remaining women were Caucasian and Hispanic, mainly of Mexican and Puerto Rican descent. Few women referred to the negative racial conditions that prevailed in the past, in the South generally or Atlanta in particular. They did not mention slavery, the Jim Crow era, the

Civil Rights Movement, or more recent examples of the on-going struggle for equality. Over the past few decades, the African American middle class in Atlanta has grown. However, the African American poor have gained little or nothing in the city. To improve these residents' quality of life, Atlanta has received various federal community development funds, such as Urban Development Action Grants, Community Development Block Grants, and the recent Empowerment and Enterprise Zone funding. In 1992, former President Jimmy Carter launched The Atlanta Project (TAP), a local empowerment initiative. One of TAP's main goals is to unite Atlanta as a community by bridging the divisions of race/ethnicity, class, and gender. However, this and similar initiatives have failed to halt the downward spiral in the quality of life for most of Atlanta's neediest residents, many of whom are women of color.

Since the early 1980s, several books have been published on the distinct experiences of African American women. Paula Giddings provided a historical perspective on the impact of gender and race in her book *When and Where I Enter: The Impact of Black Women on Race and Sex in America* (1984). In *Ain't I a Woman* (1981), bell hooks introduced an African American feminist perspective. Patricia Collins (1991) stressed the interconnectedness of gender, race, and class, a theme explored more recently by Leith Mullings (1997). Similar research on poor Hispanic and white women is lacking. At first glance, it seems that among the women in project FAST, their crack cocaine use and its consequences overshadow race and class differences. Chapter 2 will show that the women's lives varied significantly depending on their drug-use patterns and income-generating activities, independent of their class or racial background. However, it was more common for women of color to be involved with male partners who were unable to find a job or who were in prison, or to have partners or children who died in violent encounters. Social and health service providers and law enforcement officials frequently treated the women of color more disrespectfully than they treated their white counterparts. Conversely, however, the African American women appeared to be more likely to have extended social support networks and to feel confident that women can make it on their own. This strength may derive from African American history, where women had to be independent and work outside the home. Cari, an African American crack cocaine user, supported her habit primarily through prostitution. She was involved in a lesbian relationship and expressed her view of both heterosexual relationships and racial differences.

> Black women are different. We are strong, not like those white ladies. Their guy leaves them, and they fall apart. It's like it takes a guy for them to like themselves. We, we feel good about ourselves. We don't need no man to feel good. I mean, it's nice to have one, but you can feel good without one. Let me tell you something else. Black women are used to having a job. There's no staying home and taking care of the husband and the children. That has made me strong. I'm used to being out there in the tough world. I learned the hard way to speak up for myself. Most of the white sisters don't know how to make it on their own. They'd still be hiding at home if it wasn't for the drugs getting them out of the house.

Home: Family of Origin

Of the women in project FAST, two-fifths were raised by both of their biological parents for most of their lives before they turned sixteen. While several of these parents were legally married, others were involved in common-law relationships. Approximately one-third of the women grew up primarily in single-mother households. Others were raised in households headed by their mother and her boyfriend, who was not their biological father. Still others were brought up by a grandmother. A less common experience was growing up in a father's household or in foster homes. The caregiving environments of the women in this study ranged from very functional to extremely dysfunctional. Their experiences challenged the assumption that being raised in a traditional family serves as protection against social problems, including drug use.

The women's stories also revealed that household composition is a process rather than a static reality. For most of them, this composition changed several times prior to their establishing their own households. Nola, an African American woman, provided the following account of the different people who raised her.

> When I was born, my mama and my sister were living with my grandma. My mama had boyfriends, but none of them wanted to be like a father to me and my sister. She got pregnant of my brother. Now there was five of us living in a one-bedroom apartment. Grandma died, and we all had to move. My sister and I moved in with my aunt, my three cousins, and their stepdad. It was a nice house. Mama and my little brother moved in with one of my mom's friends. It was hard to be apart from my mama and my brother. Mama got her own apartment, and we all moved back together. Her old man, the father of my little brother, came and lived with us. His fifteen-year-old daughter also moved in. We were like a large family. Most of the time we got along. My brother was a real boy, and he was getting into drugs when he was only ten years old. My mama made him live with one of my aunts out in the country.

According to the women, changes in household composition affected the "house rules." For example, Penny, one of the white prostitutes, said that the rules became either tighter or more lenient depending on her mother's live-in boyfriend. Other women also indicated that live-in boy-friends had an impact on the daily routines. For example, some men immersed themselves in the role of father and wanted to set standards for the children. Others preferred to pretend that the children did not exist. Still others abused the children.

Some women had positive memories of the atmosphere in their childhood homes, though a substantial number re-called verbal arguments, physical violence, sexual abuse, and alcohol and drug use. Those women who presented positive images often had at least one adult in the house-hold who took charge. They had to obey certain house rules such as assisting with housekeeping, and they were not al-lowed to stay out after a certain time. They also discussed future plans and expectations with the adults in the house-hold. Negative experiences often involved adult caregivers who had an alcohol or drug problem. It seems that the household context, including the material and social re-sources, was more important in the socialization of the women than the composition of their households.

Three-fourths of the women in project FAST reported a drug- or alcohol-using relative. Intergenerational research on alcoholism has shown that children of alcoholics are more likely to become alcoholics or drug users than chil-dren of non-alcoholics (Boyd, 1993; Melton, 1993; Wright and Heppner, 1993). Several women in this study were in-troduced to alcohol and other drugs by either a sibling or a parent. Of those women who participated in an in-depth in-terview, siblings introduced 12.1 percent to alcohol, 22.3 per-cent to marijuana, 13 percent to heroin, and 14.2 percent to cocaine. A parent, usually the mother, introduced 12.6 percent to alcohol, 3.6 percent to marijuana, 1.1 percent to heroin, and 0.4 percent to cocaine. Intergenerational drug use did not differ by racial background.

Forty women in project FAST were either the mothers of drug-using children or the daughters of drug-using mothers. The daughters frequently blamed their drug-using mothers for their drug use and failed to take responsibility for their own actions. The mothers, on the other hand, berated themselves for failing as parents. The younger a daughter was when the mother used drugs, the more likely she was to condemn herself as a bad parent. Maggie, a white mother of three daughters who are respectively eleven, eighteen, and twenty, put it this way:

> When Sassy, the oldest, was born, I was doing fine, but I was not ready to be a mom. I got the blues, and they never went away. Two years later I had Melany, and that did it to me. Two babies was too much. I got hooked on Valium, and I picked up smoking pot like I used to do in high school. My husband left me, and I tried hard to find another man. I would do about anything to bring a man in the house. One of the guys, the father of the youngest girl, was the only one who would smoke pot with me. The oldest girls started finding out about it, and I was too high to notice they were smoking my pot. I became a crack head, and I know Sassy is smoking it, too. She won't talk with me about it, because she feels that I screwed up her life. It's all my fault.

Those women whose mothers used drugs tended to begin their own use at an earlier age than the daughters of non-using mothers. Despite their direct experience with the consequences of drugs, these daughters were more tolerant of drug use and had to overcome fewer personal barriers. More studies on motivators of and barriers to generational transmission of drug use are needed to understand the interaction between individual attributes of drug users and the impact of the household and community context.

The Neighborhoods

The majority of the study neighborhoods lie in the inner city. Much of the housing in these communities was abandoned or deteriorated and in need of extensive repairs. Often the available housing consisted of single-family dwellings and apartments, including subsidized public and Section 8 housing. The sidewalks, if present, were often in poor condition, as were most of the roads. Liquor stores, mini-marts, and car repair shops largely made up the extent of commercial and retail establishments. While the majority of the women could name stores in or near their neighborhoods, few of these businesses were large grocery stores with a variety of products, including fresh produce, for a reasonable price. Typically, the stores were small, family-run, and economically marginal endeavors.

Social and health services tended to be located outside the neighborhoods and were often inaccessible without transportation. The majority of the women resided near a bus or train stop, and many frequently used public transportation. Those women who received public assistance frequently listed free public transportation cards as a major incentive. Several neighborhoods did have a community-based health care setting, but very few women utilized such clinics. Those who did seek services at a community-based clinic felt it was a waste of their time because clinic staff often referred them to the local public hospital. To save time, therefore, they went directly to this hospital. Several women also perceived the medical care at the hospital to be more professional than at the neighborhood clinic.

Most neighborhoods had their own elementary school, but day care facilities for younger children and after-school programs for adolescents were largely non-existent. Recreational facilities such as parks, playgrounds, and basketball courts were also scarce and tended to be underutilized because of the fear of violence. Most women described social interactions between the residents as distant and secondary. They adhered to the rules of "staying by yourself" and "keeping your business to yourself." Residents who did not use drugs often preferred to stay inside their homes as much as possible, even during the hot and humid summer months. They had become prisoners in their own houses. Before crack cocaine invaded these neighborhoods, many residents used to sit and socialize on their porches. They used to look out for each other and each other's children. Nowadays, however, they are unwilling to intervene, even when the situation involves a young child.

Those social interactions that did occur tended to be superficial. The atmosphere in the neighborhoods was not one of mutual responsibility among residents but of weak social ties and control mechanisms. Several current residents envied former neighbors who had managed to move to the outlying suburbs. As the tax base of the neighborhoods dwindled, the availability of services declined and the physical and social infrastructures crumbled.

An Overview of the Study

The central purpose of this study is to gain an understanding of crack cocaine use and its consequences for women. Symbolic interaction, combined with the philosophy of phenomenology, allowed me to develop an insider's perspective on crack cocaine use, its meaning, and its consequences. This perspective also focuses on the women's social roles and the salience of these roles to the women. Mothers, for example, tended to view their caregiving role as their most salient role, but when they were smoking crack this role was often overshadowed by their role as drug users. The strain between their roles as mothers and as drug users is discussed in chapter 4.

The theoretical orientation of this study acknowledges that people in general develop images of themselves based on their perceptions of how others view and respond to them. Cooley (1909) referred to this phenomenon as the "looking glass self." The development of this image, the self, is an ongoing process in which individuals consider the reactions of others to every action they take (Blumer, 1969).

The setting—the location and the people present in it—tends to be very important as well. For example, several women in project FAST said they would only smoke crack cocaine in a get-off house, a place where users gather to get high, but never at home. Others preferred to smoke only at home. Some women smoked their supply in a short time when they were by themselves but were too embarrassed to smoke so fast when other users were present. Like people in general, the women in this study found their actions influenced by the norms and values that prevailed in the settings in which they found themselves. The anticipated reactions of others influenced them, as did their judgments of the possible advantages and disadvantages of behaving in certain ways.

A number of women described borrowing drugs from others in the earlier stages of their crack cocaine use. While some women made sure that they could reciprocate, others were unable to repay the drugs and began considering alternative ways to get crack cocaine. The negative reactions they anticipated from the individuals from whom they had borrowed led them to begin exchanging sex for crack cocaine. Constant negotiation of their roles filled the stories of many of these women. Sometimes they took responsibility for their actions, while at other times they blamed other drug users, their friends and relatives, experiences in their past, and larger social conditions.

The eight chapters that follow discuss different dimensions of the lives of the women in project FAST. Chapter 1 focuses on their initial drug use and on how their drug use patterns evolved. For most women, their initial use of drugs occurred during adolescence and included alcohol, tobacco, or marijuana. Their introduction to drugs often involved their peers, close girlfriends, boyfriends, or relatives. This chapter explores the women's reasons for continuing drug use as well as the increasing prominence drugs had in their lives. The discussion provides a detailed description of the development of the women's drug use patterns, including initial, experimental or occasional, controlled, and regular use. The women in this study became increasingly committed to their role as crack cocaine users and gradually established drug-related "careers." As they matured in their drug careers, they frequently became compulsive users.

The various patterns of the women's crack cocaine use and their income-generating activities are presented in chapter 2. Based on the women's own descriptions of their income-producing activities and the associated social roles, this chapter posits four types: (1) Queens of the Scene, women who finance their controlled habit by dealing crack themselves or preparing crack cocaine rocks for high-level dealers; (2) Hustlers, women who may or may not have used other drugs before becoming crack cocaine users and who support their habit through illegal activities other than prostitution; (3) Hookers, those women who may or may not have used drugs other than crack cocaine before becoming users of this drug and who support their habit through prostitution; and (4) Older Struggling Rookies, women who did not use drugs until they were in their thirties or older and who support their habit by bartering their bodies for crack cocaine.

In addition to being drug users, many of the women in project FAST had relationships with a significant other. Their steady relationships are the focus of chapter 3. A substantial number of women desired to be involved in long-term relationships and to be married. Their experiences include both long-term and casual heterosexual and homosexual relationships. Many were or had been single as well. Those women who engaged in same-sex relationships viewed these as less stressful because of the lack of gender-based conflicts common among heterosexual couples. For most women, the pool of available partners increasingly shrank to other drug users as their habit intensified. Apparently relationships with drug users proved more mutually rewarding than those with non-users. This chapter also examines the behavior of the women's parents as role models for their relationships and their perceptions of ideal steady relationships.

Chapter 4 turns to issues of reproduction and motherhood. The women in project FAST, like women in general, placed a high value on motherhood. They discussed many of the ways in which they grappled with reproductive decisions. Many women reported an unplanned or unwanted pregnancy despite their knowledge of available contraceptive techniques. Others believed that drugs served as an effective contraceptive. Among those women who reported the use of contraceptives during sexual encounters, condom use was most common. In reality, however, they had little control over the use of this contraceptive method because their decisions were dependent on partners who seldom sanctioned condom use.

The use of condoms tended to vary by the type of sexual partner and the context in which the sexual activity occurred. Few women had tried the female condom, but those who had used it expressed dissatisfaction with its design. A more detailed discussion of condom use as a risk-reduction strategy for HIV is presented in chapter 6.

The majority of the women in this study had been pregnant at least once. Frequently, they believed that pregnant women should eliminate or reduce their drug use, but many of them learned of their pregnancy only in the second or third trimester. Once aware of their status, several women shifted from smoking crack cocaine to drinking alcohol on the assumption that this legal substance was safer. The criminalization of pregnant drug users discouraged many of these women from seeking prenatal health care, thereby increasing the risk to mother and fetus. Once pregnant, several women chose an abortion or a drug-induced miscarriage. Some women elected to put their newborns up for adoption, and others chose to become mothers.

As is typical of most drug users, many of the women in project FAST had at least one experience with drug treatment. Chapter 5 summarizes these treatment episodes. Few drug treatment programs address the special needs of women. The major motivating factors for the women in this study to seek treatment were externally imposed directives from criminal justice staff, service providers, and relatives. Internal motivating forces included health concerns, pregnancy, and burn out. The women also identified many barriers to drug treatment, including the limited number of treatment slots for women, long waiting lists, and the male orientation of most programs, which often have no facilities for the women's children.

Those who did succeed in reducing or eliminating their

drug use often relapsed during the complicated exit process and the difficult transition from user to non-user. They valued informal support systems such as twelve-step programs like Alcoholics Anonymous and Narcotics Anonymous. The drug treatment orientations they preferred were gender-sensitive inpatient programs, combined with an aftercare program of transitional services and housing upon graduation. Such programs, they believed, take a holistic approach by addressing all aspects of their lives.

Chapter 6 deals with the AIDS epidemic and its consequences. Since the 1980s, the epidemic of AIDS has challenged the biomedical community. Researchers have discovered that women who use crack are at risk for HIV infection because of sexual activities, which often involve unprotected sex with anonymous, multiple partners. Although the majority of the women in this study had heard of HIV/AIDS, many of them were misinformed about risk behaviors and risk-reduction strategies. Those women who claimed to have implemented behavioral changes to reduce their risk often referred to intentions rather than actual changes.

This chapter also includes a discussion of issues surrounding HIV testing. The self-reported HIV infection rate among the women in this study was 10 percent. Only a few of the women sought the test voluntarily and usually underwent testing upon an arrest, entrance to drug treatment, or admission to a medical setting. Many women preferred not to be tested because there is no cure for AIDS. They also feared legal repercussions if they were found to be HIV positive. The biggest fear among the mothers among these women was losing custody of their children.

Violent encounters were common in the lives of the women in project FAST, and these experiences are the subject of chapter 7. Violence has become an integral part of U.S. society. Our rates of violence are higher than those of any other industrialized country. Available studies reveal a complex relationship between drug use and violence. Frequently, researchers explain violence among and by drug users by examining the psychopharmacological effects of the drug, the outcome of crimes committed to support their drug habit, or the inherent presence of violence in the drug world. This tripartite model ignores cultural factors, such as gender role expectations, and developmental issues—including childhood abuse experiences—and structural forces such as poverty and racism.

This chapter includes a comprehensive overview of the violence experienced by the women in this study. Their encounters with violence included childhood and adult experiences. As adults, violence pervaded their lives in domestic settings, in drug-use settings, and in their communities. The final section explores the link between violence and HIV risk-taking. The women's experiences with violence and abuse often allowed them to deny or ignore their HIV risk-taking behaviors or hindered them in negotiating safer behaviors.

Chapter 8 deals with the women's perceptions of the past and the present and their aspirations for the future. The Older Struggling Rookies were most proud of their past accomplishments and the Queens of the Scene of their current circumstances. The impact of the constantly changing drug market on the women's experiences is also discussed. In addition, the chapter presents the women's opinions on possible ways to improve the quality of their lives. Many women acknowledged that societal changes were needed to reduce racism, poverty, and sexism, but they also described actions they could take themselves.

Finally, this last chapter addresses the potential implications of the legalization of narcotics like crack cocaine. Legalization would remove legal sanctions, which in turn might enhance the quality of life of drug users. Opponents of legalization often fear that it might attract new users, especially among the young. However, the negative reputation of crack cocaine as a destructive drug and the increasing diversity of the drug market might prevent them from becoming users. One thing seems certain, and this is that future studies need to go beyond individual-level explanations to focus on the intersection of personal characteristics, household dynamics, and community factors in explaining drug use, addiction, and possible remedies.

Harm reduction will only work if placed in a larger context.

1 Getting Into Drugs

Different pathways led the women in project FAST to their current drug-use patterns. Getting into drugs often involved others, typically a close girlfriend, a boyfriend, or a group of friends. Marijuana was the first illicit drug that some of these women used. Others began with snorting cocaine, injecting cocaine and heroin, or immediately smoking crack cocaine. Angel, one of the white women who supported her crack cocaine habit through street prostitution, described hanging out with her friends and smoking her first marijuana as a teenager. At first, she and her friends reserved getting high for special occasions. Within several months, however, she needed to take a few puffs on her way to school. Lisa snorted cocaine for many years before she shifted to smoking geek joints, a mix of crack cocaine and marijuana. She recalled going to dance clubs with her best friend and being intrigued by the cocaine snorting that took place in the restrooms. Before they knew it, they were pooling money to buy a few grams every weekend. Gail, one of the African American women who had ambitions to become a drug dealer, first got high when her boyfriend injected her with a speedball, a combination of heroin and cocaine. Long after this relationship had failed, she still was injecting drugs. Angel, Lisa, and Gail all were crack cocaine users, but the ways in which they became involved with drugs differed dramatically.

30

Most women in project FAST experimented with tobacco, marijuana, and alcohol during early or middle adolescence. Despite the breadth of available studies on drug use and its consequences, initiation into drug use has received relatively little attention. According to the women in this study, however, their initiation was an important life event, and many vividly remembered their first use.

Not surprisingly, many women experimented with drugs during their adolescent years, a time in the life cycle when young people begin developing their own identities and distancing themselves from their parents, while associating more and more with peers. A substantial number of women explained that as adolescents they often felt misunderstood and disrespected by their adult caregivers. They responded by "acting out," which could mean isolating themselves at home, skipping school, running away, becoming pregnant, or experimenting with drugs.

Friends were seen as individuals to whom the women could relate and who seemed to have similar interests. Among friends, these women explained, they did not feel as anxious about their popularity. Anna, who left home at the age of fifteen because of difficulties with her mother and her stepfather, recalled:

> I must've been fifteen. Things weren't going well. My mom's boyfriend didn't like the way I dressed. He told my mom I looked like a hooker. She didn't really mind my clothes, but with him in the house she had to say something. We would just fight, and I started hanging out at my friend's house. I'd stay out really late. They'd make me stay home, but never for long, because of the fighting. I quit doing my homework. The teachers told me it was a shame because I am a pretty smart woman. I'd buy liquor with my best friend, and we'd get wasted. Her boyfriend always had pot. I ran away from home

when my parents got tough . . . one of my friends became
pregnant and they freaked out.

Lisa, who came from a middle-class family, also recounted having problems with her parents and other adults
during her adolescent years. Her social class failed to insu-
late her from troubles similar to those encountered by Anna.

> I am the bad one in the family. My parents made it all the way.
> They wanted me and my brother to do even better. My brother
> went to medical school, and he is a surgeon. I was never good
> enough, so after a while I quit trying. All I would get from my
> parents were bad feelings. My teachers told me that I was not
> good enough . . . I felt like a nobody. My friends didn't care
> about me not being good enough. I started arguing with my
> parents and my teachers and using dirty words, like I was from
> the street. The kids at school would accept me the way I was. I
> made new friends, kids from outside my neighborhood. I had
> some money, and they had the connections. I took my first
> acid when we went to a movie.

These women's negative attachment to their parents and
teachers was a risk factor for their drug use. Other researchers have also identified this risk factor (Kandel, 1975;
Newcomb, Maddahian, and Bentler, 1986; Schulenberg
et al., 1994). A second major risk factor for the women in
project FAST was having peers who supported their drug
use. Several women described feeling alienated from home
and school due to their involvement with a boyfriend. Often these boyfriends introduced them to a way of life that
was supportive of drug use.

Tobacco, Alcohol, and Marijuana

The median age at which the women in project FAST
smoked their first cigarette was fifteen, with the youngest
woman being five years old and the oldest twenty-one.

Only a few of the women had never smoked tobacco. A majority grew up in households in which at least one person smoked, and sometimes this person introduced them to cigarettes. More typical were stories of women who began smoking cigarettes with friends. Some women recalled that if enough peers were interested, they would pool their money to buy a pack of cigarettes. Despite legal restrictions on tobacco sales to minors, none of them had trouble buying cigarettes.

Many women also reported having tried alcohol for the first time during adolescence. On the average, most women consumed their first alcoholic beverage at the age of fifteen, with the youngest woman reporting her first alcoholic drink at the age of seven and the oldest at thirty-three. As with cigarettes, some women were introduced to alcohol at home, while others had their first alcoholic drink with friends. Several women remembered drinking alcohol for the first time at a birthday party, wedding, or funeral. Teranda, an African American woman in her mid-twenties, experimented with alcohol when she was fifteen. She and her girlfriend sneaked some of her mother's supply.

Alcohol really wasn't that big a deal in my community. We had more liquor stores than grocery stores. All the old guys would be standing on the street corner with their brown bags and be getting high. Me and my friends would make fun of them. I didn't really know my mommy was getting high. For me, alcohol was something in a bottle, in a brown bag. She kept hers in a locked cabinet in her room. She tells the story that I got drunk one time when I was little. My granddad had passed, and all the relatives were over at the house, and I would go around and take a sip. My girl friend and I were snooping around in my mom's room and we found the key to the cabinet. We was drinking her vodka or rum or something and telling how delicious it was. I didn't like it one bit, but, of course, I had to make it seem as if I loved it. Most kids at my school were getting high, and I knew some of the guys would be drunk before they came to school in the morning. Alcohol was part of the community, and I got into it because that's what we did. After a while, I even started liking it . . . I remember it making me less shy with the boys.

Other women recounted similar experiences. Few of them had been warned about the potential negative health consequences of tobacco or alcohol use, but many remembered being cautioned about marijuana. Most took their first marijuana hit with their friends. As the literature shows, new users often experiment with drugs in the company of their friends, because they consider them trustworthy (Biernacki, 1986; Coombs, Fry, and Lewis, 1976; Hughes, 1977; Waldorf, Reinarman, and Murphy, 1991).

Several women were socialized to view marijuana as an acceptable substance. Often, their parents were current marijuana users or had used the drug in the past. Many of these parents were white and middle class. Linda, who is in her early twenties, talked about having her first marijuana experience with her mother, who is in her mid-forties.

Me and my mom are very close, and she really is a cool parent. For years I didn't want to give her credit for being cool, because teenagers are not supposed to say that adults are cool. If it wasn't for her, I probably would be pregnant or have a baby. She was really good about respecting me but still helping me not hurt myself. She smokes pot, and one day she let me have her joint. I knew all along about her smoking pot, but she always thought she could hide it from me. Us smoking pot together was like a bonding thing . . . we'd do it when the little kids were out of the house. My mom told me that pot was illegal and all that stuff. She explained that smoking pot was a thing of the sixties.

Linda was not the only woman whose parent smoked marijuana. However, parental use of marijuana did not necessarily translate into a tolerant attitude toward the women in this study when they began to partake of the drug, especially among those whose parents no longer smoked it. Several women called their parents hypocrites for prohibiting them from smoking marijuana, when they had previously or currently used it themselves.

The women in project FAST told numerous anecdotes about their first marijuana use, often recounting that they did not know how to inhale or exhale or what they were supposed to feel. Howard Becker (1953) has documented that many first-time users fail to get high because of their lack of knowledge and skills. Several women feared they might embarrass themselves when they were stoned. Melinda, a crack cocaine user who started smoking marijuana regularly as a junior in high school, remembered being unable to get stoned because of such worries.

> I always knew that sooner or later I would start smoking reefer because almost all my friends smoked it. We were at this one guy's house, in the basement, and all of us were talking about being high. We'd be passing a joint and I would pass without taking a hit. I was nervous that I would make a fool of myself. I'd see people change, like they'd be emotional, say what they had on their mind, or crawl around or something weird. I remember taking a hit and keeping the smoke in my lungs. All I could think about was keeping my cool. I must have been thinking so much that I never got high. Once I learned how to relax and stuff, I started getting high.

Almost none of the women remembered fearing that they would become addicted to marijuana. Most of the marijuana users they knew seemed to have control over their habit and their lives. Once their curiosity was aroused, several women sought out situations where marijuana was likely to be present. Melinda, for example, attended only those parties where she knew marijuana would be available. It is uncommon for new users to have their own supply and, as other researchers have demonstrated, one of their main concerns is gaining access to the drug (Binion, 1982; Coombs, 1981; Marsh, 1982; Rosenbaum, 1981; Waldorf, 1973).

The question why some women experiment with and continue to use drugs, while others with similar backgrounds do not, is complex. Many women in project FAST explained that their continued drug use frequently depended on coincidence, on "being in the right place at the right time." Other women, however, took more responsibility for their continued drug use and, like Melinda, actively sought out situations where drugs would be available.

Most of these women seemed to have made a deliberate decision to continue using drugs, though they themselves preferred to present their reasons for doing so as accidental. Regardless of individual circumstances, all of the women in this study continued to use illicit drugs and became crack cocaine users. Linda, whose mother introduced her to marijuana, described her transition from marijuana to crack cocaine use as coincidental.

> I started smoking pot when I was like fifteen or sixteen. It wasn't a big deal. It didn't really get in my way. I think that pot should be legal. At a party someone gave me a joint with some crack laced in it. I was the lucky one because I hit the rock. It freaked me out, like you feel everything at once. I wanted more, but my friends told me I should be careful. . . . I would have someone else buy my crack. He was a guy whom we all knew, and he had connections for all drugs. I would not go out—just stay in my room and smoke crack. Or I would smoke some, and my friends would tease me because my eyes looked all spooky. My friends just came out and told me they didn't

want me coming around with this crack stuff, and I started
hanging out with Derek and his friends. They all smoke rock.

The social context in which Linda was using marijuana
opened her to crack cocaine. Her friends at the party made
the drug available and approved of her trying it. When she
continued to use crack cocaine, however, she had to identify individuals outside her social network to gain access to
the drug. Ultimately, she no longer associated with her old
friends but surrounded herself with other crack cocaine
users.

Several women limited their illicit drug use to marijuana
for years. But as they began smoking marijuana more frequently, their friendship networks often shifted from both
non-users and users to users alone. In addition, they increasingly identified themselves as drug users. In other
words, their identity as drug users began to overshadow
their other social roles. Symbolic interaction theory refers to this process as the shifting of prominent roles.
Penny, who supported her crack cocaine habit through
prostitution, recalled that she did not mind giving up her
old friends, being expelled from high school, and losing
her job.

> Most of my life has been about drugs. I am about drugs. That
> needs to change by me becoming a mother, you know [she
> was pregnant at the time of the interview]. I know I need to
> quit if I want to be a decent mom. I started with a joint, like
> once in a while. Next thing I know, I'm stoned about all the
> time. I got kicked out of school for having pot on me. My best
> friends from kindergarten stopped talking to me, and I just did
> not care. I got a job at a pizza place. I can't even remember
> why it happened, but I got fired. It's crack now. Like I'm sup-
> posed to be a drug user. You remember I told you I wanted to
> cut down and be a good mom? That's scary. Like, I'd have to
> become a new person.

Like Penny, all of the other women who enrolled in project FAST were crack cocaine users. The rest of this chapter focuses on their cocaine use.

Trying Cocaine

Women who used other illicit drugs prior to their experimentation with crack cocaine often referred to those earlier experiences as preparation for their crack cocaine use. The drug literature sometimes refers to marijuana as a gateway drug or a stepping stone to other drugs.[1] One has to keep in mind, however, that the study design for project FAST excluded women who did not move on to crack cocaine.

The women's experimentation with cocaine tended to begin at an older age—in the late teens and early twenties—than their introduction to tobacco, alcohol, and marijuana. Several women used another form of cocaine prior to becoming crack cocaine users, with intranasal use being the most common intermediate step. Teranda, the African American woman who at the age of fifteen used alcohol to gain confidence, smoked marijuana on only a few occasions. By the time she reached the age of eighteen, some of her friends were snorting cocaine.

> You have to understand. I never had anything against drugs. I used to think that it's the people who don't know when to stop using and not the drugs that make problems. I mean, how could I say, for example, that I was better than a person who smokes pot or does some other drug? Alcohol is not much better. Drunks can be nasty. Just cause it's legal doesn't make it better. I was surprised when I found out that some of my friends were snorting cocaine, but that didn't make me not like them or something. If you want to know the truth, I wanted to try it myself. I wasn't very impressed with it, but it created a

bond between us. Just to have some together, not like a habit or anything. Only trying it out.

Teranda learned that the effects of intranasal cocaine use are not always easily recognized by inexperienced users. Several women didn't know what to expect from snorting cocaine, and they were often unsure whether they had felt the optimal effect. Some wondered if they experienced an effect because of the cocaine itself or because they were excited about trying the drug.

The introduction to cocaine for a number of these women involved crack cocaine. Marta's boyfriend introduced her to cocaine when she was thirty-five. At that time, she had been smoking marijuana for almost two decades.

> I am no saint. I smoked joints all my life, but I never would do anything else. My old man was into cocaine. He always kept it out of the house. I don't know exactly what happened. About a year ago, he started bringing it into the house. I was upset, but then he let me try some. He told me we would be partners. That's really how it all started. At first, he'd only let me snort lines. That fucking didn't do much other than make you feel like you were gonna get a bad cold. I didn't think it was great, but I wasn't gonna tell him. He'd cut me off from having any more. I finally got to do some rock. That took me a while too before I liked it. It made me feel like I was gonna get a heart attack. I learned that I can enjoy it better if I have a few drinks or roll myself a joint, like a dessert, after rock as the main course.

Whereas Marta had no difficulty recognizing the effects of intranasal cocaine use, she had to adjust to the effects of crack cocaine. Only a few women were unable to detect any effects from smoking crack cocaine. Alice, whose story was presented in the introduction, described her first crack cocaine high as follows:

My hands already were wet from the excitement, but soon they were even wetter. I took a hit, like sucked it in really quick and let it make its way to my brains. It didn't take but a minute. I could feel my heart beat getting faster. My eyes and my mouth went dry. I was sweating all over . . . my muscles were all tight, but it didn't hurt. It's like you get to go to heaven for a second. No kidding, I thought I was gonna die, but a pleasant death.

Those women who were familiar with the effects of marijuana often were surprised by the different effects of crack cocaine. They also noted that while marijuana use typically occurred in a group context, where joints were passed around freely and people watched each other get high, crack cocaine was much less social. Tashia, a white hustler in her late twenties, smoked marijuana before trying cocaine. She pointed out that cocaine users were more secretive than marijuana users.

I knew they were using drugs. One of the girls told me it was cocaine, but I didn't believe her. I thought that only movie stars and rich people used cocaine. You had to be kind of approved before you got in with the cocaine users. . . . They always thought they were slick. Like one person would get up, and go into the other room. That person would come out, and after a while, someone else would go in. My friend asked me to go in with her. She had asked me before, but I always would give her an excuse. I mean, at the time, I thought marijuana was okay, but cocaine was too much for me. None of the cocaine users acted like they had a bad experience in the other room. Actually, it seemed to put them in a good mood. They'd be talking and dancing . . . I figured it couldn't be that bad. The time I finally had some, she put some cocaine on my lips and my tongue, and I could feel it. She also put some on my teeth or something. I snorted a line, and I was waiting for it to hit me . . . it was like nothing. My friend told me cocaine is a subtle drug. Heck, I liked marijuana a lot better. Once I was into cocaine, I told other folks it was great, and they believed me. To tell you the truth, I still like marijuana over cocaine.

A number of women did not experiment with any other illicit drugs prior to trying crack cocaine. In contrast to their peers, they lacked a reference point. Brenda, who started smoking crack cocaine at the age of thirty-three, described her first experience.

> First of all, I was in denial. I knew about people's lives getting messed up from the rock, but I still wanted to try it. I wasn't an addict, so I thought it would be different for me. Like I could try it just once, so I could know what was so incredible about it and never use it again. I never considered I'd be a crack addict. I asked my best friend if she would smoke a rock with me. She had been telling me that many folks use it without becoming addicts. We sat down together. First she took a hit, and she gave me the pipe but she did not put a new rock on the screen. She told me to inhale the smoke, she said that was safer. I know she was ripping me off. . . . The first time was a real spiritual experience for me. Now I need a rock so I can keep on going. It went from crack making me feel good to crack being the medicine for the pain I caused myself to have.

Special Occasion, Experimental, and Controlled Cocaine Use

After their first introduction to drug use, people have the choice of never using drugs again or of continuing use. All of the women in project FAST continued to experiment with cocaine and became occasional users, meaning that they only used cocaine on special occasions or at times when cocaine was readily available.[2] The time lapse between first and subsequent use depended on the women's evaluation of their initial cocaine experience as well as their access to the drug. After their first experience, one in five women did not snort cocaine again for a period of six months, while another two-thirds did not snort cocaine again within three to six months. Those women whose first cocaine use involved crack cocaine frequently tried the drug again within two weeks, a much shorter time period than for other drugs or other forms of cocaine. The time periods for initial and subsequent use of cocaine by injection fell in between. Sandra, an African American crack cocaine user, initially had cocaine only when her friend visited her. She related the following about her use during her friend's visits.

> Cocaine is a fine drug. It doesn't mess with you like heroin does. I like what it does to me. Most people didn't know I was using at the time. I'd get high every time my friend came into town. We'd go to this other friend of ours. He always knew where to get good cocaine. It was like a special thing for us to do. At the time, my friend was shooting up the cocaine, but that always scared me. We had this routine for about five years. I didn't miss getting high when she wasn't around, but I needed to have some as soon as she walked in my apartment.

Women like Sandra only used cocaine when they experienced a "trigger" or "cue." Other cues described by the occasional users included being at a party where the host was known to be a cocaine user, attending certain concerts, or having pleasant memories of their experimental use. Some individuals pursued cocaine use more actively. Like Melinda, in her efforts to find marijuana, they sought out parties where cocaine would be available. Valerie remembered being opportunistic with all her drugs.

> I was so uncool. I'd be inviting friends over at my place, because my mom always had to work nights. As soon as they'd walk into the house, I would ask if they had some. One of the guys liked me a lot, and I started dating him only so I could get my hands on his reefer. I began taking speed, and I'd use the same game. I'd always have an excuse to get some—the same with heroin, the same with cocaine. All my life, I have been

planning how to get dope for free. I could have paid for it, but I told myself that only addicts would pay, and I did not want to be an addict.

Many women in this study referred to crack cocaine as a drug for which controlled use was difficult. Even women who had previous experiences with heroin or cocaine injection agreed that controlled crack cocaine use over a prolonged period of time was hard. Marsha, who starting smoking crack cocaine at the age of thrity-two after injecting heroin and cocaine for more than seven years, gave her opinion of controlled crack cocaine use.

> Before I got into rock, I was like an old-timer who loved the needle. I still like shooting up much better. The high is much more smooth, and you know you are getting high. Smoking crack hits you right away, and you keep on chasing that first high. It's a drug that lets you get high only one time. The next time it doesn't feel as good, and you just chase a feeling. Chasing makes it so you can't control your habit.

In their chronological accounts of cocaine use over time, these women described a pattern from first use, to occasional and experimental use, to controlled use. "Controlled use" meant a higher frequency of use but not necessarily an addiction, they told themselves. While the women still viewed their use as experimental, their use pattern indicated a higher level of commitment. Angel captured this progression.

> Cocaine . . . okay. I did the whole thing: sniffing, popping, and smoking. Every time I figured I could stop when I wanted to. That's what control means. A person may get high every day, but if they can stop, they control their habit. Like they still are trying to find out if they really want to be a user. It happened with me, but really I wanted a better high all the time. I was sniffing about a gram a day, and my nose was stuffed all the time. I needed a better way and started skinpopping. That way

> I could tell myself that I was controlling my habit. A person
> doesn't pop as much as when you sniff it. Next thing, I am
> mainlining . . . my veins are in bad shape . . . I smoke some,
> and I shoot up some, and I fooled myself all along. I'd be
> telling myself I was in charge of my habit, and that I was trying
> to find out which way was the best for me.

Other women confirmed that while they viewed them-selves as experimental users who controlled their cocaine intake, they had moved beyond experimentation into regular use. Many women acquired their own drug paraphernalia and developed their own connections with a dealer. Most women in project FAST confirmed the "pipe line" metaphor, the movement from occasional and experimental use to regular use (Kaplan, Bieleman, and TenHouten, 1992), but the pipe line for crack cocaine was a short one. The women's drug histories revealed that once they began using crack cocaine, they became regular users of this drug within a relatively short period of time. A study of cocaine users in Amsterdam found no evidence that cocaine users lose control over their habit and become regular or com-pulsive users (Cohen, 1989). While this is the case for some cocaine users, only a few women in project FAST, the Queens of the Scene, fell into this category.

Regular Use

Initially, most women in this study relied on their friends' cocaine supply or on taste samples from dealers. Sooner or later, however, they were confronted with the limits of their suppliers' generosity. In addition, as cocaine use increas-ingly dominated their lives, they needed a larger supply to stay high. For several women, the craving for cocaine started to occupy most of their thinking, and they increased their use to cope with their craving. Some women also indicated that they seemed to have confidence in themselves only when high on cocaine. The increased role of the drug in their lives may result partly from the psychopharmacology of cocaine, but it may also depend on the increased importance of their social role as cocaine users. Most women remembered the importance of developing their own contacts with cocaine dealers and acquiring personal paraphernalia, especially a crack pipe.

A number of researchers have compared the development of drug-use patterns and the corresponding formation of social roles with the building of a career. Traditionally, the career perspective has been applied to lawful occupations, but it also has been applied to deviant activities such as drinking (Wiseman, 1970), prostitution (Bryan, 1965), and drug use (Faupel, 1991; Rosenbaum, 1981; Waldorf, 1973; Waldorf, Reinarman, and Murphy, 1991). Typically, deviant careers tend to be less linear and more chaotic than traditional or lawful careers.

The process of starting a career as a cocaine user required that the women be willing to continue to use cocaine, and that they had either direct or indirect access to the drug. Without making a conscious choice, the women became increasingly committed to their new role and shifted from novices to regular users. Melinda, the crack cocaine user who earlier in this chapter described having to learn how to smoke marijuana, became addicted to crack cocaine much more quickly than she had become a regular user of marijuana.

> Crack is different. It kinda takes over. Marijuana lets you think
> about what you are up to. . . . Sometimes, I needed some
> badly, and I'd be thinking about how to get more. I'd always
> find a way. Sometimes I could borrow some from one of my

associates or I'd figure out some other way to get it. At one point, I was smoking every day, in the morning, in the afternoon, and at night. . . . With crack, I wanted to try it. Everybody talks about it and I am the kind of person who needs to know what it feels like. The next day, I went and got myself another hit from my friend. The day after that I gave her ten bucks and asked her to go buy us some. She finally introduced me to her dealer. At first she didn't want to, because I was giving her some of my rock for getting it. The day I found out where to get it, my habit got bigger.

Other women realized they had become regular cocaine users once they started worrying about ways to support their habit. Some women who initially snorted cocaine began injecting the drug to experience a high with a smaller amount. Once they injected, the frequency of use often increased, again in order to get high and to cope with the craving. As their veins collapsed from frequent use or as their fear of AIDS increased, many moved to smoking the drug. Others did so because they thought this route of administration would be cheaper. Many women learned that they were unable to control their habit. Dollar, one of the African American hustlers, related her experience.

I have gotten so stupid, I can't fucking believe it. When I was snorting lines, I'd just put it in my nose. I didn't care if I was wasting it. It was the thought, the expectation of feeling something. I was wasting it because I was going though my supply too quick. You want to use as little as possible to get high. You can't go getting higher than high, but your mind messes with you and tells you that maybe you should try some more, reach a little higher. If I run out, I can just sit there, and I think about getting high. Some folks told me that they can feel high just from thinking about it. Like when I crave for a rock, I can make myself feel the effects of the next rock I'm gonna smoke. This sounds kind of crazy, but that's how you fool yourself. That's what is wrong with crack heads. We never know when to stop.

2 Patterns of Income Generation and Drug Use

The continued use of crack cocaine by the women in this study gave increased prominence to their role as drug users.[1] The low unit price has made this type of cocaine more affordable than cocaine in powder form, and thus available to a larger segment of the population. Prior to crack cocaine, the smallest sales unit of cocaine, typically one-half of a gram, sold for twenty-five dollars. Sold in rock form, however, it can be purchased for as little as five dollars, sometimes even less. Many of the project FAST women, however, soon discovered that a cheap high from crack cocaine quickly translated into an expensive habit. A major drawback of crack cocaine, they found, was the very short high, which lasts only a few minutes and is followed by an almost immediate craving for the next rush. The following field notes capture one of my observations of a group of people who were smoking crack at Sir's place. His apartment was not a public crack house but served as a gathering place for a number of his friends. He seldom supplied the drugs. Instead, his friends would bring rocks or cocaine powder and share it with him and each other.

> Lynn, Sir's girl friend, walked in with several grams of cocaine. Nobody asked her how and where she got it. As soon as she

put it on the table, Sir took charge and told her to take half of it and put it away. Lynn appeared to be an expert at cooking rocks from powder. Nobody smoked, or even talked, while she prepared the rocks. Sometimes she would stop and make sure everyone was watching her. As soon as she handed the rock on a plate to Sir, the silence stopped. Everyone began talking. Some began cleaning the pipes. Others made sure there were cigarettes and beer. In many ways, this gathering felt no different than being at a party where everyone is excited about the uncorking of a bottle of champagne. Sir assigned the smoking turns and soon the atmosphere changed. He took a hit, leaned back, and peacefully stared at the others while they smoked. Lynn soon couldn't sit still and was walking around, agitating the others with her constant chatter about nothing. After a few rounds, the rock was gone and the focus shifted to discussions about the powder in Sir's pocket. The tension rose, everyone crashed from their wonderful highs and all they could talk about was getting high again. All the stash was gone. The friends were arguing. One could feel the craving in the room.

Sir, Lynn, and their friends were always in need of money to support their crack cocaine habit. Lynn estimated that some days she spent close to one-hundred dollars, but she always made sure that she first paid her bills and had money for food. When asked about their finances, the women would often shift the focus from how they afforded their drug habit to the challenges of paying for necessities such as lodging, food, and clothing for themselves and, in the case of those women who were mothers, their children. Economic survival was often a problem long before they used drugs.

Most women had limited opportunities to earn sufficient money through legal means. Those women who were legally employed tended to be in their thirties or older, and they were often newcomers to crack cocaine use. A number of the African American and Hispanic women had jobs as domestic helpers, office cleaners, or factory workers. Among the white women, the most common employment was in the fast-food industry. The scarcity of such food establishments in the inner city neighborhoods where most of the women of color resided may account for this difference in type of employment. In general, few of the women in project FAST participated in the formal employment sector at the time of the study, although approximately two-thirds of them held a lawful job at some point in the past. As crack cocaine began dominating their lives, those women with jobs were either fired or resigned because they were no longer able both to do their work and to continue using drugs. They often found more attractive job opportunities in the underground economy.

Another formal income source used by almost half of the women in the study was public assistance or welfare. A number of women, especially those who grew up in welfare-dependent households, had no experience in the employment sector and few intended to pursue a job since none were available, anyway. Recent welfare reforms require an increasing number of recipients to seek employment, but many of the welfare-dependent women had young children and were not affected by the new requirements.

Other women relied on public assistance only when their job opportunities dwindled. Mary, who began smoking crack cocaine after she moved into a drug-infested neighborhood, strived for economic independence, but at times still had to rely on welfare.

> It seems like I have done it all. My resumé would be very long, but it's not what you'd call impressive. I've been a waitress and a maid. For a few years I worked in the pencil factory, always the evening or the night shift. The money I made really wasn't

worth it, but it was a job. I got fired from several jobs because
of the kids. The only job I ever liked was with a cleaning company. I had to do three floors in this office building. The people
whose office it was moved, and the company laid me off. When
things started getting tough, like right before pay day, I'd have
to go in the store and steal food. A friend got me into stealing
checks. I didn't have to sign. I'd give the checks to him, and
he'd pay me for them. We also did credit cards. I've had welfare about three or four times. Every time they give me some
useless training, and one time they helped me find a job. These
are my certificates, but they don't get you a job. What they
teach you may be important, like how to look for a job and to
feel good about yourself but it don't do much when you need
a buck.

Several women participated in job-training programs,
self-esteem classes, and related courses, but generally these
courses failed to create more opportunities for them. For
those women who did find legal employment through a job
training-program, the length of employment tended to be
limited and the pay low.

Because of their drug use, society often views women
like the ones in this study as undeserving welfare recipients
(Abramovitz, 1988; Edelman, 1988; Sidel, 1986), but statistics on the relationship between welfare status and drug use
reveals that most women who had received public assistance at some point in their lives did so prior to becoming
involved with drugs. Independent of their drug use, many
women faced a daily struggle to survive and to stay out of
poverty. They lacked access to employment opportunities
that would provide economic independence. Their dependence on welfare prevented several women from increasing
their crack cocaine use. For example, to be eligible for public assistance, recipients have to attend regular meetings
with their case workers, and they must maintain a legal,

local home address. Because of such requirements, some women in this study organized their lives in such a way as to avoid missing appointments with their case workers and gave priority to paying their rent.

Many welfare recipients, Mary among them, complained that the level of support was insufficient, and that they were forced to rely on additional sources of income, both legal and illegal. Examples were unreported jobs in the informal sector, such as domestic work, and jobs in illegal sectors, such as prostitution and the drug business. For many women, reliance on illegal sources of income increased as they became more involved with crack cocaine. Several women, however, used the additional income for daily necessities as well as for drugs. Sandra, a thirty-two-year-old mother of three, earned additional income through various hustles.

> I hustle on the side, and I smoke rock, but I am also a mom. I may not be a good one, but I try to do my best. I get high when the kids are asleep, or sometimes I take a hit when they are playing outside the house. Like I'll sneak into the bedroom and take a quick hit. I have my hustles to pay for my own dope, and my children won't hear that their mommy is a hooker. We need the extra money. I don't just use it for myself. I make sure that once a month the kids and I go see a movie, and we go to a restaurant. It is important for them. My boy wants a new jacket really badly. I am tired of telling him no, so I'll make my own money to get it for him. You can't go to your case worker and say, "Oh, my poor son, he'll become a criminal if you don't help him." They don't care. They can mess with me, but not with my kids. I know how it feels if all you hear in life is no, no, no.

Like Sandra, other women also used their illegal income both to support their drug habit and to pay for household needs. They expected to continue to need such income, even in the event that they stopped using drugs. A few of the women acknowledged that if they quit using crack cocaine and other drugs, they might be more motivated to seek legal jobs that could distance them from illegal activities. At the same time, these women expected to need unreported income from legal jobs to support themselves and their families.

For all of the women in project FAST, drug use became a way of life, their "master status" (Hughes, 1945). Along with other drug users who encouraged them to embrace drug use, they increasingly began to identify themselves as drug users. To maintain this status, they turned more and more to illegal means to fund their drug use. The women paid for their drug habit through a myriad of activities, including drug dealing, "cooking" (the preparation of crack cocaine rocks from cocaine powder), and other criminal activities, including prostitution.

Based on the women's stories, I developed a typology that acknowledges a hierarchy in their economic support strategies and the importance of the social context of the women's crack cocaine use, including the frequency of use, the settings, and the people present. The four main categories in this typology are: Queens of the Scene, Hustlers, Hookers, and Older Struggling Rookies. The Queens of the Scene were women whose drug use, including their crack cocaine use, is limited and who typically support themselves by cooking rocks for a dealer or by dealing crack themselves. Most of the Queens of the Scene in this study were younger African American women. Women primarily involved in illegal activities other than prostitution were the Hustlers. They often had tried other drugs prior to crack cocaine and represent all age categories and racial backgrounds. Hookers were those whose main hustle was prostitution. They also often used other drugs before becoming involved with crack cocaine, and they spanned all age and racial groups. The Older Struggling Rookies were the women whose first illegal drug experiences occurred when they were in their thirties or older. They often lacked skills to support their drug habit and turned to bartering sex for crack.

The Queens of the Scene

The general stereotype of women addicted to crack cocaine portrays them as willing to do anything for a hit of crack, including selling their bodies for a small amount of money (Inciardi, Lockwood, and Pottieger, 1993). The Queens of the Scene, however, failed to fit this stereotype. They considered themselves part of the drug aristocracy and therefore superior to other women involved with drugs. In the crack cocaine world, they were accorded a high status because they either possessed the cooking skills to transform powdered cocaine into rocks of crack or were involved in high-level drug dealing. Their role as cooks reflected gender expectations regarding the division of labor in mainstream society. Several women joked that this role was gender-appropriate, as cooking is a common female activity in western societies.

The women saw cooking rocks of crack cocaine as prestigious for a number of reasons. It provided them with direct access to upper- and middle-level dealers rather than the lower-level street sellers of prepared rocks. Furthermore, the cooking required special characteristics such as concentration and patience (Williams, 1989). Cooking crack cocaine rocks from powdered cocaine is a complicated process, and one mistake can cause the cocaine powder to go up in smoke (Sterk-Elifson and Elifson, 1993). The cocaine suppliers and high-level dealers actively sought well-qualified cooks to increase their financial profit.

In addition to having technical skills, cooks had to be able to regulate their drug intake because of their continuous access to powdered cocaine and crack cocaine rocks. The suppliers and dealers, most of whom were men, expected the female cooks to refrain from getting high while working and to curtail an extensive drug habit during working hours. Several women in project FAST explained that once cooks become obsessed with getting high, their cooking skills decrease and they tend to make mistakes. More important, a cook over her limit could be tempted to use drugs on the job, steal drugs from her boss, or increase her habit.

Employers protected good cooks, treating them as valuable commodities. Sean, who only transacted business with middle-level dealers, spoke about one of the top cooks in his safe house, which processed countless pounds of cocaine into rocks.

> She is quite a lady . . . damn, she knows how to do it. You know, always just the right amount of baking soda and the right temperature. You see, I am convinced that you ladies have a special touch for cooking. It is something more than just learning what to do. She is my baby, and I'll do anything to keep her happy. She can always take time off as long as she prepares enough supply in advance. I tell her she should snort, and not smoke. You see, once the craving gets in the way, she is lost. I have seen that happen too many times. When I feel like she needs a treat, I'll take her into a hotel room, and we freebase it together. She can get high, but she can't become an addict. She has asked me to pay her with powder, but I'd rather buy her a nice fur coat. I respect her, and she knows she can pull one over me because she is so good. That's all part of it.

Other dealers who employed cooks shared a similar admiration for them, emphasizing the women's ability to contribute to their economic well-being. If they learned of unauthorized crack cocaine use by a cook, however, they would fire her on the spot. During informal conversations, several employers explained that cooks sometimes become overly distracted by their habit and begin engaging in activities other than cooking to sustain it. A number of cooks buy crack cocaine on the street to hide their increasing use from colleagues and employers at the safe house, and this can place the business at risk. One dealer recounted how one of his former cooks lost control of her drug habit and shared business secrets with outsiders, including other high-level dealers and law enforcement officials. There is an unspoken rule in the drug hierarchy that the aristocracy should have no interactions with "riff-raff." If cooks violate this rule, they often find themselves on the street. However, only one woman in project FAST experienced this pronounced downward mobility as her career shifted from prestigious cook to prostitute.

Based on their power and control as cooks, these women occupied an unusual position among female crack cocaine users. They tended to be the most powerful and independent and the least likely to be poor. Most Queens of the Scene were in their twenties, which suggests that age may be a factor in a cook's success. The women offered various explanations for this age bias, including the younger women's physical attractiveness, greater ambitions, higher energy levels, and the propensity to "show better in public" during business gatherings. Most of the Queens of the Scene were African American, but a few were white. One African American dealer who employed several cooks always made sure that he had a few white women among them. When asked for an explanation, he said it was part of his marketing strategy. He wanted those white people with whom he did business to see that he had some white women among his cooking staff. He also said that, at the personal level, he felt that having white women work for him enhanced his power.

On several occasions, dealers offered me a job on their kitchen staff. While most of these offers were made in a joking way, some dealers used subtle pressure to encourage me to consider the offer. In one instance, described in the following field notes, I had to exclude a dealer and his female cooks from the study sample because of such pressure.

> T.'s place is becoming uncomfortable. His jokes about me cooking rocks for him are no longer funny. We used to laugh about the idea, but his comments are making me nervous. He seems to get angry when I don't respond and just laugh. I don't want to go back to his place. It doesn't feel safe. We ran into each other and he wanted to know why I hadn't been by to visit. I fed him a bunch of excuses, and I guess he realized I intentionally was staying away from his place. He got upset. When I asked if it still was okay for me to come by and do an interview with one of his cooks, he responded, "Only if you pay me back. I already told you about the sweet deal I have for you." I told him, in that case, I had to cancel the interview.

On several subsequent occasions, T. and I spoke with each other, but I never asked him again for permission to conduct interviews, and he never mentioned my involvement in his business. We both realized we had exhausted our options for collaboration.

Whereas the dealers appreciated the cooks and viewed them as valuable assets, they also felt threatened by them. Several bosses developed strategies to prevent the women from becoming too powerful and frequently relied on macho games to equalize the relationship. These power games included threats to replace the women with a new cook or requests that the women provide free sexual services to them or their business associates. Men commonly used sex as a weapon to gain and maintain control over their female employees.[2] Several cooks said that once their employers perceived them as gaining too much power, the frequency and severity of sexual harassment and intimidation increased. Rose, a twenty-seven-year-old cook with at least four years' experience, described the tension between herself and her male employer.

> We went through this a few years ago. He was afraid I would be leaving him, and I would play with him. I think he never got over that. A man is not supposed to beg a lady for anything. He could not have this business without me, and he knows it too. It's driving him crazy. First he tried the other girl thing, and I told him to fucking go ahead. He figured out that wouldn't work, so next he wants to be on top of me. Don't get me wrong. He is a nice guy, and we are like partners. But you see, sex puts a man on top of the woman. It makes them feel like they own you, like you are their pussy cat.

Rose acknowledged that she provided sexual favors to keep her position. She rationalized these favors by their common frequency among business partners. Such favors are integral to the party-like atmosphere among high-level dealers, users, and cooks, according to Rose. More than one-half of the cooks provided sexual services for their male employers, but did not label these interactions as sex-for-drugs exchanges. Typically, the men refrained from requesting sexual favors until the women had worked with them for several months. As one woman said, "By then they know you love the job and everything that comes with it." A few of the women feigned weakness and hid their self-confidence from the men to avoid being perceived as a threat. Such strategies included acting less well-informed and secure than they actually were and appearing uninterested in the business. While these ploys prevented the women from being perceived as threatening, they failed to free them from having to provide sexual favors.

Several women further raised their status by becoming drug dealers themselves. In her study of drug dealers, Adler (1993) described women's involvement in drug dealing through their alliances with men, a pattern that held true for almost all female dealers in project FAST. Freda had been running her own high-level business for almost eighteen months. She described her approach.

> I'm telling you a woman can do it without a man looking over her shoulder. It's like business executives. There's not many women in those positions, but the women who have an executive job often are better at it than their guy colleagues. It's the same in the drug business. A lady dealer is more in touch with her customers. She'd listen to them when they have a problem, asks them how they are doing, and is willing to give them a break when they need it. Yeah, I need protection, but I pay my guys just like everybody else does. You're making a mistake if you think that only big guys can run a business. Things have gotten very competitive, and just one strong guy is not enough to keep the business from getting bought out by the competition. Every high-level executive dealer has people around to protect the business. My guys are proud to be working for me.

In their research on female crack sellers, Eloise Dunlap and Bruce Johnson (1996) found that women were more attuned than men were to their customers' needs. Jeff Fagan (1994), in his study of 311 women, found that they were involved extensively in drug selling and that this was inversely related to prostitution. He also noted a significant disadvantage for women in the gender-biased drug business.

Recently, four other women in project FAST began their own operations independent of local high-level dealers, thereby opening new doors for local Atlanta women in the drug world. Freda, along with the other high-level female dealers, stressed the importance of keeping a low profile. They believe that women are more discreet than men, who are socialized to "show off." Compared to the drug business in marijuana (Goode, 1970; Fields, 1984) and heroin (Johnson et al., 1985), women apparently have more opportunities in running their own crack cocaine business.

The Hustlers

The Hustlers were those women in this study who engaged in a wide range of criminal activities to support their crack cocaine use. Typically, they thought of these activities as their work, and they occupied a substantial part of their daily lives. Sheranta, who grew up in Puerto Rico and New York City before moving to Atlanta, described herself as an experienced car thief. She described an average day in her life.

> Most of the time, I get up around noon, and the first thing I see is my pipe or a roach [the butt of a marijuana joint]. I smoke the reefer and try to wake up. I take off my dirty clothes and wash up at the sink. As soon as I am dressed, I figure out what part of town is good for the day. Like if there's a fair or street market or if the Braves are playing in town, that's where you go. If nothing is up, I may walk through downtown or go to the mall parking lot. Once I get to my spot, it takes me a while to figure out the scene, find my cars, and figure out the security schedule. It takes me at least three hours to get the job done. I don't smoke crack when I'm working. My first hit will be around five or six in the afternoon, and I'll smoke until I pass out. If I run out of money, I can always get some because people know I'll pay them back the next day.

While Sheranta's schedule varied, her days were relatively structured, and she divided her time between work and drugs. Other women described a similar pattern. Although drug use and criminal involvement seem related, research exploring a causal link is inconclusive (Johnson et al., 1985; Gandossy et al., 1980). Researchers have shown the drug-crime connection most clearly in studies among male heroin users. Until the 1970s, investigators largely ignored the involvement of women in drug use and criminal activity. Even those studies that explored crime among female drug users often had a limited focus on shoplifting or prostitution (Inciardi, Lockwood, and Pottieger, 1993). Relying on studies of male users, many researchers assumed that female users turned to crime to support their drug use. The stories of the women in this study, however, indicate that many engaged in criminal activities prior to using drugs.

The Hustlers in project FAST often had a history of criminal involvement dating back to their adolescence, the same life stage during which most of the women became involved with drugs. Their most common criminal activities were motor vehicle theft, shoplifting, and pickpocketing. Fewer women committed crimes like robbery and burglary. Most women specialized in at least one crime to take care of their business.[3]

The women expressed mixed opinions about the drug-crime link. Some viewed their involvement in criminal activities as part of their drug-use role, while others separated the two activities. One woman hinted that she expected to continue her criminal activities even if she ceased using drugs.

> I'm not sure how my drug use and my hustles go together.
> Booting [shoplifting] and fraud are my main hustles. Some-

times I'll get into something else, like a burglary, but that's
only if I am asked to be a partner. I use the money I make for
rock and heroin. I blow it all on drugs. I don't think I would
become a citizen with a nine-to-five job if I quit doing drugs. I
use the money for dope, but it is the excitement of having a
good hustle that I like. I'd still be doing it, with or without
drugs.

Other researchers have supported a subcultural connection hypothesis, which postulates that drug and criminal
subcultures often intertwine because of the illegal nature of
the activities of both groups (Gandossy et al., 1980). According to the women in project FAST, the dynamics surrounding the linkages between drug use and criminal involvement are much more complex than is often assumed,
and one should look beyond the order of involvement. In
addition, their criminal activities ranged beyond traditional
crimes, and also included quasi-crimes related to the drug
business. Some women were "runners," individuals responsible for supplying street dealers with drugs and, if necessary, transporting the rocks across town. Others served as
"holders," persons who keep the drug supply for the street-
level dealers, or "steerers," who refer potential customers to
specific dealers. Bruce Johnson and his colleagues (1985)
have identified a similarly wide range of distribution roles.

The Hustlers in project FAST believed that they were
more likely to be arrested for traditional crimes such as car
theft and prostitution than for drug-related crimes. Once
the police knew them, their chances of arrest increased. For
example, law enforcement officers often harassed a number
of women known to be involved with car thefts as they
walked past or stood near a car, even though the women
were neither involved nor planning any illegal activity. The
women's experiences challenge the assumption often made

by researchers that an increase in criminal involvement, measured as an increase in arrest, symbolizes an increase in drug use (Ball, Schaffer, and Nurco, 1983).

A number of the Hustlers used crack cocaine in combination with marijuana or injectable heroin and cocaine. Most runners, holders, and steerers used only crack cocaine and tended to be more committed to crack culture than were their peers who also smoked marijuana or injected drugs. The social networks of women who used only crack cocaine, especially their drug-use network, often consisted exclusively of other users of this drug, while the women who used other drugs maintained social and drug-use contacts outside the crack cocaine world. In addition, women who used other drugs in addition to crack were more likely to engage in crimes unrelated to the drug business.

Several women made more income from criminal activities than they spent on crack cocaine. While some women used the surplus to build up their savings, others invested the extra money in crack cocaine they then sold for a profit. Frequently they shaved some crack from the rock but charged full price. Among heroin users, these jugglers or small-time dealers were often viewed as part of the distribution network (Goldstein, 1981; Johnson et al., 1985). A number of female jugglers in project FAST viewed this role as a stepping stone to a higher-level distribution position, even if their ceiling would probably rise no higher than assisting middle-level dealers.

The Hustlers in project FAST frequently attributed their success to their social and technical skills. Liz, an African American crack cocaine user, engaged primarily in shoplifting and in steering potential users to a dealer. She described the importance of her shoplifting skills.

You can send me on any mission, and I know that it will work. I can't tell you all my tricks, but I get people to trust me. I don't dress like a slut, but I also don't overdress. Women think that security [guards] look for what you are wearing. Let me tell you, that's not the case. It's your attitude that matters. You want to come across as a customer who is actually wanting to buy something but who needs some privacy to decide if it's worth the money. Clothing stores are my favorites, although I also started getting into computer stores.

Women like Liz are successful because of their flexibility. Their opportunistic traits allow them to take advantage of the world around them. Their skills include "street smarts," the ability to detect a plainclothes security guard or police officer, and knowing how to recognize optimal hustling situations. The women's main hustle typically combines several different talents, including technical and social skills and street smarts. As they did for Liz, these skills become an important part of their identity.

Many women in the study faced a dilemma. Their expertise and the greater earnings associated with it allowed them to increase their drug habit. However, to succeed in their criminal activities, they had to maintain control over their intake. Recall Marta's description in chapter 1 of her introduction to crack cocaine after twenty years of marijuana use. She worried that deeper involvement with crack cocaine might lead to her arrest.

Hustling is not as easy as it seems. It can give a person a nervous breakdown. You can always get caught. It makes me nervous. When I was younger, I used to like that feeling, but now it scares the fool out of me. It's not that I have been busted. I'm just tense about it. Maybe it is because I have started doing more cocaine. I shoot it up, and I smoke it. It messes too much with my mind. If it wasn't for getting high, I wouldn't be hustling.

Most Hustlers disapproved of extensive crack cocaine use because it negatively interfered with their criminal activities. Increased crack cocaine use forced other women to earn more money. Their involvement in criminal activities actually helped them control their habit. Frequently, they identified themselves as Hustlers first and drug users second. While all of the women in the study wanted to continue their drug use, they also desired a nice wardrobe, a new car, and expensive jewelry. Natasha, a white Hustler in her late twenties, engaged primarily in check fraud and shoplifting. She hoped that her earnings would support her crack cocaine use and allow her to purchase luxury items. Natasha also connected her criminal involvement to her self-image.

> Yeah, I need to hustle, but don't you think it is only so I can get high. Getting high is important to me, but it's not the only thing. I want to look like a lady. That's why I have some nice clothes, and I get my hair done every week. That's important to me. It's like another addiction. I need designer clothes and some nice jewelry to go with it. I don't like flashy as much as I like quality. My car is another example. I am the only woman I know around here who has a Camaro. My house is a mess, but I never meet folks at my place anyway. I've seven credit cards, and sometimes I have to hustle extra or borrow money to save myself from a penalty. Hustling is part of my life. It's for the drugs, and it's for me.

Many Hustlers aspired to become cooks or middle-level crack cocaine dealers. Gail, an African American women in her late twenties whose hustles resembled Natasha's, contemplated a career move in the drug business.

> I take care of myself, and it is my responsibility to make sure I have dope or get the money to buy some. I used to shoot up, first heroin, but later only speedballs. It is a better feeling for me. Sometimes I smoke ready rock, or I'll cook up a rock my-

self. I know these few guys who are up on top. I mean, they
don't sell their stuff to street folk. You have to buy a few
pounds or kilos. I got to know them on my missions [success-
ful criminal activity that brings in money]. If you want powder, you get a better deal when you buy more, and only guys
who know business sell powder. I have been thinking about
working for them.

Women like Gail dealt with middle- or high-level dealers
because they bought cocaine hydrochloride from a private
source rather than cocaine powder or crack rocks from public dealers on the street. She and women with similar ambitions sought to impress their dealers, hoping for a job offer.
They emphasized professionalism in their interactions with
the dealers. A number of dealers responded by creating
opportunities for them, and several women added drug-
related crimes to their income-generating activities. J. J.,
who became involved in petty property crimes as a teenager
and started using crack cocaine in her early twenties, was
one of them.

> I got started shoplifting when I was in high school. There was a
> group of us. We'd go out together. If one of us scored a good
> deal, we'd all be excited. At the time I didn't think about me
> doing drugs. I used my money for clothes, albums, and stuff.
> One of the guys I dated smoked reefer, and I would smoke
> with him. . . . I wasn't an addict until crack. That shit gets ex-
> pensive. People out here know that I know business. I always
> steal things that sell for a decent amount of money. I never go
> below the price I should get for something. I'd rather trash it.
> My neighbor, he's a big time dealer, asked me if I was interested
> in helping him. Within a few months, I became his best per-
> son. I sell more rocks than any of his other workers, and I have
> not been arrested even once. I want to meet his boss, because
> I'm too good at it to do my business through him. He knows it,
> and it scares him. He is hoping for me to sell my pussy so he
> can put me down. I will never do that, that's too low. You have

to plan when you go out to hustle and when you get high.
Most people don't plan, and that's why they go under.

Most Hustlers agreed that it was difficult to break into the circle of middle- or upper-level dealers. The dealers kept their networks closed to protect themselves from competitors and law enforcement. They also preferred to keep some distance between themselves and their workers. Employees such as cooks, lower-level dealers, runners, holders, and steerers were supposed to look up to them. For women to be admitted to a drug business clique, they had to demonstrate first that they would adhere to the unwritten house rules. As one dealer explained:

> We're all in the same business, and there's a lot of competition
> out there. It's okay for a dealer to expand his territory and take
> over a dealer who can't defend himself. A dealer who puts
> everybody's business at risk won't make it. One guy called the
> police on another dealer and had his people waiting to take
> over as soon as the police took the dealer out. Snitching gets
> you killed. Some of the ladies are good at selling this shit, and
> they get away with more. It's a pain for the cops to search
> them, and they don't want the hassle of calling a lady cop. One
> lady dealer fell in love with a guy who was the competition of
> her main man. She told him some business secrets, and it
> screwed up things. With women you have to watch out.
> They'd forget the business if they fall in love. Maybe not all
> women, but this one bitch did.

Other male dealers confirmed the need for trust. Many dealers in one neighborhood spoke of a local woman who breached her dealer's trust, stealing the dealer's business with the help of her boyfriend. Although several of the dealers interviewed for this study did not know this woman personally, each one had a story about her. One said the woman steered potential buyers to her boyfriend. Others said the boyfriend's friends broke into the dealer's place. A number of dealers used this one example repeatedly to support the assumption that women are less reliable once they become romantically involved, especially if the lover is an outsider. They commonly feared that a woman's commitment to the group could be easily overshadowed by an intimate relationship. Consequently, male dealers often prohibited women who worked for them from dating someone outside the group. Because they were viewed as a potential business risk, these women often had to demonstrate more commitment than their male counterparts.

While several Hustlers moved up the drug-career ladder, most were less successful. To support their drug habit, they had to combine their hustles with prostitution. For Suzie, one of the white women, prostitution was a last resort.

> Selling my body, that is the last thing I want to do. It depresses me, and I feel like a fuck-up. I got involved with this guy who needed someone in his business. He gave me the rocks up front, and I didn't have to pay him until later. I was making a lot of money that way. I know I am a good salesperson. I started smoking too much myself, and one day I didn't have any money. I didn't want to go to my man because I was afraid he would kick me out of the business. I had to give head for hours to make up for the money I spent.

Women like Suzie initially viewed prostitution as a temporary solution to financial troubles. They resorted to prostitution in times of despair but otherwise generated income from less demeaning hustles. Richard Stephens (1991) documented this roller-coaster effect of the ups and downs of the drug business. More often than not, however, prostitution shifted from being a marginal support strategy to being the women's main hustle.

The Hookers

The Hookers were those women in the study whose main hustle was street prostitution. Street prostitution is not unique to crack cocaine users, of course, but it is a common way for female drug users of all types to support their habits (Goldstein, 1979; James, 1976; Miller, 1986). Several women worked as prostitutes before they began using drugs, including crack cocaine. Frequently, they became involved with drugs because of their easy availability in or near prostitution strolls. Drug use as self-medication also resulted from the stress associated with prostitution.

Other women in the study used drugs prior to becoming prostitutes, and they often turned to prostitution to fund their drug use. While experts agree that prostitution and drug use appear to be linked, the dynamics of this relationship are complex. Most Hookers were involved in prostitution activities prior to the emergence of crack cocaine on the drug market. Frequently they traded sex for money, which they used in turn to purchase drugs other than crack cocaine. Typically, they were socialized to accept the norms and values common among non-using street prostitutes.

With the emergence of the crack cocaine epidemic, however, a major shift has occurred in the prostitution scene. Whereas clients traditionally have paid street prostitutes in cash, prostitutes who use crack often trade sex directly for drugs (Inciardi, Lockwood, Pottieger, 1993; Sterk, 1990). The prostitutes in project FAST who had previously used drugs other than crack cocaine remembered soliciting customers in public settings and having sex with them in hotel rooms or in the customer's car. They negotiated in advance both the type of sexual service to be provided and the price. Once they became crack cocaine prostitutes, they often met and had sex with their clients in crack-use settings. Frequently, they accepted customers indiscriminately and failed to agree in advance upon a reasonable price for the sexual services. In addition, they sometimes engaged in uncommon sex acts, including sexual performances with another female.

The behavior of the Hookers was largely related to the setting in which the sex transactions took place. Inside a crack house, for example, women often had difficulty refusing customers or turning down sexual requests. When working the stroll, they rarely used drugs in the same settings where they traded sex. Numerous other researchers have confirmed this finding (Cohen, 1980; James, 1976; Perkins and Bennett, 1985; Sterk, 1990; Zausner, 1986). Sue, a white woman who worked the streets for nearly four years, and who had recently begun working in a crack house, captured these differences.

> On the street you would never touch another lady's man, even
> if he is trying to charm you. Every woman has her spot and
> her guys. There isn't that much competition. Like once a girl
> walks up to the car, you stay away from it until she is gone.
> You also ask about the same price as the other girls. It's not like
> we have a set list like in a hair salon, but you kind of know
> what to ask for. Most of us also refuse kinky sex. Now if you
> go over to L Street, you know you can get kinky sex. . . . It's
> a little like a family—in a crack house anything is possible.
> Women fight over the same guy, and they'll do anything. They
> give head in the middle of the room, and you see two women
> blowing bubbles [having oral sex with each other]. I have
> heard of places where they use animals, but I have never been
> in a place like that. The guys totally control the women.

Other women concurred that prostitution in a crack house was very different from that in any other setting. Several Hookers who did not work in crack houses refused to accept the "crack whores." Cari, an African American woman in her early thirties who had earlier expressed her pride in the strengths and independence of African American women, said:

> The only thing that makes them be called a whore is that they sell pussy or give blow jobs. To be a prostitute you need to have pride and know the rules. The geek heads will freak with anybody, and they will do it anywhere. They suck them guys, and they even suck each other. This is not prostitution or pornography. It is sick sex.

Among the women in this study, those like Cari, who exchanged sex for money, were less common that those who provided sex for crack. Crack cocaine use narrowed women's options. Marsha Rosenbaum (1981) described the same phenomenon among female heroin users.

Many women expressed the opinion that "any woman can sell her pussy." Some of these women traded sex for crack cocaine for several weeks, or sometimes months, before they began to think of these exchanges as prostitution. Rita, a twenty-nine-year-old woman who has used crack every day for the past four years, explained how she was prostituting herself without identifying her actions as such.

> It's not like I want to be a whore. I never thought about it, but I got into it. I guess it happened once I started smoking crack. The guy who introduced me to it used to be a friend, but he ain't no friend no more. He and I would get high and have sex. Before I knew it I was giving other guys blow jobs only so I could get my next hit. I didn't even know those guys. I never got money for it, only pieces of rock. I used to think that if you don't get money it ain't no prostitution. I wasn't doing no drugs before crack. I never stole anything from the store or did any sin. Any woman can give sex. That's what I ended up doing. It's not a hustle because I give more than I get. A hustle means you are good at it, and you can make money off it, like

stealing checks or something. I'd like to do something better than hooking, but I am always high.

Many women failed to recognize that they were prostituting themselves until they were faced with a situation in which no male customers were available. As one woman said:

> I never had any trouble. There'd always be some dude who would have me suck his dick for a hit. I'd never plan how I was gonna get high because it always kind of happened. I got at the house right after a raid, and almost no people were there. I sat around waiting for a guy. I finally got the guts to smile at one of the guys, but he winked at another chick. It hit me hard . . . here I was, wanting to get high, but no guys around to help me out.

Several women described similar experiences, coming to the realization that they lacked bargaining power. One woman remembered:

> I was hitting on this guy because I knew he just bought some. He'd just look at me and joke around with his buddies. He called me over, and he wanted to know what I had to give him. I didn't have anything to say. He told me that the guys thought I wasn't good at blow jobs and some other things. I started crying and watched them smoke and have sex with some other girls right in front of me.

Most women agreed that sex-for-crack exchanges required fewer skills than other forms of prostitution and other hustles. Tina, an African American woman who used to shoplift and work as a street prostitute, described what happened to her.

> I had my hustles down. I always shifted between stealing expensive dresses from the store or walking on B Street. I was good at both. If the cops were putting on the heat, I'd stay off the street, and I'd go shopping. I'd never go back to the same store if the same security guard was working. You won't be-

lieve me, but I had my routine down. Crack came along, and I'd wear myself out getting high. I looked so bad I couldn't go into the stores I used to rip off. Even my tricks commented on my appearance. It was much easier to turn tricks in the house. Now that's all I have. I can't go out and do what I used to do because all I can think about is my pipe.

The context in which crack use and crack-for-sex exchanges occurred tended to be chaotic. Typically, the women in this study had enough money to buy at least one or two rocks. Once they started coming down from their high and had no money, however, they would start looking for a man. Male drug users typically paid for sex with a rock or a cloud of smoke in a glass pipe. Non-using men, who visited crack houses to purchase what one of them called "cheap sex," typically made their payments in cash, with reimbursements ranging from three to five dollars for oral sex and from five to ten dollars for vaginal sex.

Some women requested that the sexual activity take place in a relatively private setting, such as behind a curtain, in the bathroom, or around the corner in a stairwell. However, as they became known as crack prostitutes, they often found it increasingly difficult to request such privacy. Consequently, the women's craving for crack led them to engage in public sex, most commonly oral sex with a man or another woman.[4] The recruitment of male customers often became problematic. Once a woman developed a reputation as a crack prostitute, most men stopped respecting her.

A number of women preferred to engage in sex with men who did not use drugs, mainly because of the likelihood of a cash payment. Also, these customers were not distracted by their own craving for drugs, nor plagued by the frustration associated with drug-induced impotence. Tina again:

I would say the straight guys are a pain. They tell you what they want, and they are cheap because they know you are an addict. They are very arrogant, and you can tell they disrespect you, like the way they grab your head and pull it down. You can't even take a break . . . that's true. A guy who uses is fun as long as the supply lasts, and a smart woman would get away before he runs out of rock. The problem with them is that crack makes them aggressive and impotent. That's not my problem, but he thinks it is. I guess they all are a pain, and a woman always has to protect herself or get high and not care for that matter.

The link between crack and sex among women has received extensive attention (Inciardi, Pottieger, Lockwood, 1993; Ratner, 1993; Williams, 1992). Women who have been socialized into the world of prostitution on a sex-for-cash basis appear better able to maintain their social identity as prostitutes than those whose prostitution has always been linked to crack cocaine use. The crack-addicted Hookers tend to view themselves as crack users who trade sex to support their habit rather than as professional prostitutes. Their social-structural location places them in a more vulnerable position than that inhabited by women with an independent history of prostitution.

The Older Struggling Rookies

The Older Struggling Rookies are a unique group of prostitutes and represent a new category among female drug users. They are women who never tried drugs before beginning to use crack cocaine at age thirty or older. They tended to have neither a previous drug history nor a history of participating in illegal activities. Instead, they often led "regular" lives as partner, mother, or colleague, and conformed to traditional gender roles. Most Older Struggling

Rookies in this study lived on the margins of society, often in public housing. Many were unemployed and saw their opportunities as severely limited. Margie, who started using crack cocaine at the age of forty-two, reflected on her life prior to her involvement with crack.

> I've never had much in life. I came from a poor family in Alabama, and my great-grandparents worked as slaves. My mom had seven children, and I was the second oldest. I never got to meet my father. She told us he was dead, but then later I found out he left her for another woman. I started working for white folks when I was fifteen. They had a daughter about my age, and it was very difficult. I had my first baby when I was sixteen. I wanted to get married, and the baby's father still is my only real love. I've had other guys since then, but it never worked out. Like I'd be the one working and taking care of the kids. There's no jobs for guys, and that makes them feel beat down. I was living in my mom's house, but it burned down a few years ago—something about an old electricity system. I had no insurance, and me and two of my grandchildren moved into the complex. I always made sure the place was clean, and the babies always had nice clothes and stuff. Their mom had a nervous breakdown, and she is in some kinda institution. I've always been poor, but I ain't dirty. I always made sure that people talked about me as a proper person. I used to work in the church all the time, and people in the complex would come, and ask me to help them out. I was like a leader. Sometimes we'd barely make it, and I'd have to borrow some money from the pastor or someone. I bought new outfits for the kids because I knew my check was coming in. It was stolen, and we went kinda broke. I cried for the first time in a long time, and the lady who lives next door let me smoke her pipe.

Women like Margie were very concerned with social approval. Because they lacked economic resources, any negative event created a crisis. Some Older Struggling Rookies became involved with crack cocaine when they were unable to cope with a divorce or a breakup with a significant partner. Others lost their jobs and faced long-term unemployment. These disturbing events often involved situations over which they had little or no control. Mary started smoking crack after she moved into a crack-infested neighborhood.

> It all happened way too fast. The house was my mother's, my grandmother's, and my great-grandmother's. None of us had the money to keep it up, but we'd try to fix things up as much as we could. The city inspected it, and they told me what to do to get it approved. I couldn't afford it, and we had to move out. I got a little money, but that didn't stretch far. I had a hard time moving into a new neighborhood. I was used to knowing everybody, but I am a stranger around here. The lady next door helped me move in, and she seemed nice. One hot summer night, she lit her pipe, and she told me to have some. We did that several times, and next thing I know, I was buying crack myself.

Crack cocaine provided an escape from everyday life for women like Mary. It allowed them, temporarily at least, to cope with daily stresses. These women had no difficulty purchasing crack cocaine because of its ready availability in their communities.

Other Older Struggling Rookies were introduced to crack cocaine by their children. Kate, a forty-five-year-old woman who cared for her grandchildren, recently lost her job and her apartment. She said:

> It doesn't make sense—why am I doing this to myself? The business closed, and I couldn't pay the rent. I wanted to stay in the same school district, so we moved into a bad area. It was the only place I could afford. The kids were scared, and they wouldn't go outside. My daughter came by once a week to see the kids. A few months ago she and I smoked a rock together. She said it would make me feel better. I would never give her money because she blows it all. She can come and get a meal or a bed. I started giving her money so she could get some-

> thing for both of us. That didn't last long because she would
> smoke it herself. I had to go out and get it for myself. A
> woman my age should know better, but I couldn't help myself.
> I can't even tell you the things I do to get that stuff.

Drug use as a form of self-medication evolved into an unaffordable addiction for these women. They did not initiate their drug use to seek pleasure. Nonetheless, their position was extremely vulnerable because they lacked the skills to survive as drug users. They had no "drug smarts," no "street smarts," and they lacked experience with criminal activities.

Initially, many Older Struggling Rookies could support their drug habit with their savings or by selling their belongings. In the end, they exhausted their resources, and the only way they could survive in the drug world was through prostitution. However, as most of these women were less physically attractive and sexually experienced outside monogamous relationships than the younger generation, they frequently had difficulty finding men who wanted to exchange crack for sex with them. The following is a segment of Amy's life story. Three months after this interview she tried to commit suicide and was admitted to a mental hospital.

> I can't tell you about it. I'm at a place where I thought I'd
> never be. For years, I fought against becoming a bad person,
> and here I am . . . I can't even look at myself anymore. I never
> sit down and think about my life and where I should be going.
> It's too painful. I hadn't had sex for a long time, and now I'm
> acting like a whore. Black people don't do the oral sex like
> white folks do. Now, I am doing it with guys I don't know.
> They tell me I'm ugly. They disrespect me in my face. I cry and
> beg them for help. These guys are rude. I'm not gonna be able
> to take this much longer.

Men looking for cheap sex often viewed the Older Struggling Rookies as easy targets. These potential customers held unreasonable expectations, demanding sex for little or nothing. In addition, these "male partners" tended to be aggressive, impatient, and frequently impotent due to their own crack use. The drug culture accorded both the women and their partners a low status. Ray, a male crack user who prefers sex while getting high, said:

> It is pitiful. It's a shame. You have those old chicks who don't know if they are coming or going. They have no idea of what is going on. A guy is nice to them, and he gets a ten-dollar job for one hit. It is wrong, people shouldn't have to live like that. The guys can't get a hard-on, and they get after the women. We watch for physical violence, but there's nothing we can do about what it does to the women's soul. The men who can't get any other chick and the women who can't find any tricks just find each other.

While these women were older and tended to have extensive life experiences, they remained rookies in the drug world. Their experience failed to socialize them for the world in which they came to operate. They were not committed to their drug-use role, and they did not identify themselves as crack cocaine users. More than any of the other women in this study, they experienced difficulty in negotiating their social role as drug users.

The Older Struggling Rookies experienced a total loss of self. Existing theoretical perspectives on deviance fail to explain the position of these women and do not consider the larger social, political, and economic context in which they live. Crack cocaine use by Older Struggling Rookies seems to represent a social problem rather than a criminal act.

3 Significant Others

THE WOMEN'S STEADY SEX PARTNERS

The women in this study had both heterosexual and homosexual relationships, relationships built on love and on pragmatism, long- and short-term relationships, and relationships with both drug users and non-users. Most of the women in project FAST felt that their drug use placed them in a position of social isolation. Mainstream society labeled them as women who deviated from gender-role expectations by engaging in illicit behaviors, including their drug use and the ways in which they supported their habit. Among drug users, they often held marginal positions as well. The stereotype of female crack cocaine users as women who exchange sex directly for crack cocaine rendered them "unfit strangers" (Lofland, 1969) and undesirable steady partners. At the time of the research, a limited number of these women were involved in steady relationships, few Queens of the Scene and no Older Struggling Rookies among them.

Typically, the Older Struggling Rookies were single prior to their involvement with crack cocaine. While many blamed themselves for the chaos in their own and their family's lives, they also listed the devastating impact of poverty and racism as contributing factors. Kate cared for the children of her daughter, a crack cocaine user. She had recently begun using crack herself and gave her view of this situation.

I'm now almost fifty years old, and I think I have had almost
anything bad happen to me that could have happened. A
grandma is supposed to help her children and grandchildren,
but I am smoking crack. I always wanted a man and a nice
marriage, but men my age are either dead, in prison for life,
or struggling not to become homeless. Government is destroy-
ing the black family because they can't stand it that we were
strong together.

Other studies have corroborated the findings of this
study (Belle, 1982; Gibbs, 1990). The pool of available
steady partners for most women in project FAST, including
the white and Hispanic women, tended to be limited to men
who were drug users. Marsha Rosenbaum (1981) relates
similar findings for the female heroin users in her research.
In chapter 1, the women in project FAST described how
their entrance into the crack cocaine culture caused their
reference group to narrow to other drug users. They increasingly felt uncomfortable around non-users, and their
non-using relatives, friends, and acquaintances began to
distance themselves from them because they disapproved of
drug use.

Several women were involved with non-using steady
partners during the early stages of their drug-use career.
Relationships with non-using partners were often problematic and less mutually rewarding. As the women's use pro-
gressed, such relationships tended to fail as both partners'
social worlds lacked sufficient overlapping connections. In
relationships with steady partners who also used drugs,
many women hoped to avoid having to hide their drug use
or being challenged about it. Others never tried to develop
a steady relationship with a non-using partner because they
believed that as "bad" women they did not deserve "good"
men. Overall, the ability to share drug experiences with

partners appeared most influential in the women's selection of significant others, despite their yearning for love and happiness.

Being With a Male Non-User

Only a few women, mainly Hustlers and one Queen of the Scene, had a significant other who did not use drugs. These women did not expect the relationship to succeed unless they could quit using drugs. Some women hoped that relationships with non-using steady partners would motivate their own efforts to become drug free. Others, however, held more pragmatic views and stressed advantages such as not having to share their drug supply and having access to greater financial resources than they would enjoy with drug-using partners. Mantley became a Hustler when her husband filed for divorce out of frustration over her inability to stop using. She described the ultimate collapse of her three-year marriage with a middle-level local business manager.

> He was a few years older, but he seemed much more mature. He always talked about how he wanted something good out of life. He was very business-oriented and on top of everything. He was a good provider for me. At first, he didn't know about me doing drugs. We met at this place called Fat Falls. It's like a bar, but a nice bar. He would come around after work, well-dressed and really classy. I have always been attracted to people who can have a good conversation and who can talk about something other than sex. Sometimes he would come sit next to me. We liked each other, and both of us would talk about just about anything. He liked to talk about the latest news in the paper. I never read the newspaper, but I caught myself reading the headlines on my way over to Fat Falls so I

could drop a line or two. He cried when he found out I was
snorting and smoking cocaine. I was getting sloppy and spending too much money. I always knew it would be a matter of
time before he would find out. He got into this mission to get
me off drugs. That was very sweet. I mean, he could have
dumped me right there. It's just that I wasn't ready. He didn't
trust me anymore, and he became very possessive. Next, he
got into babies, and he would say, it would be much easier to
forget about drugs if I would be pregnant and have a child to
care for. I didn't want to lose him. I tried very hard. I promised
him I would quit. I promised myself I would quit. But I wasn't
ready. He gave me an ultimatum. I had till my twenty-fifth
birthday. You won't believe this, but I got very high that day. I
knew it wouldn't work. He left, and he hoped that I would be
so sad that I would quit. I started using more. Finally, he asked
for a divorce.

Women with stories like Mantley's often referred to increasing tensions in their relationships. If their partners
were unaware of their drug use, they constantly feared being discovered. Most of them smoked crack at home only
rarely and planned their highs carefully. One of the advantages of crack cocaine, a few women found, was its relatively short high, but their craving remained problematic.

In addition, the women with non-using partners were
often concerned about ways to support their habit. Even if
the household budget was such that they could afford to
buy drugs, they feared that high expenditures might raise
questions. Frequently, shoplifting was their main hustle.
Sherry, one of the white Hustlers, was married for almost
six years to an attorney before he began to suspect that
something was wrong.

We met at a business meeting. They had a big exhibition, and I
was there to help out a friend. Because we had name tags, we

could go to the reception. Man, it was mighty fancy. I looked very slick, like I was the business type: nice dress, nice jewelry, not garish or like a whore, but very classy. He caught my eye, and I told my friend, "Honey, that's Mister Right." I knew he had his eye on me, too. It took forever, but he walked over. I was being very shy, but he seemed to enjoy that. The sucker! He gave me his card. I told him I didn't give out my phone number. Just think—he would call my place while a bunch of us are getting high! I waited like three weeks. My friend kept on pushing me. It became like this thing I had to do. We set up a date, and he picked me up in the lobby of one of the nice buildings downtown. You see, I had to come up with a place that wouldn't make him suspect anything. I made him believe that's where I worked. The dress I wore, I stole that afternoon in a nearby store. That was pretty chancy, but it worked. He had to travel all the time for his job, and he badly wanted a house and a woman. He wanted to move fast, and that was fine with me. We were married in three months. I told him I wanted a private wedding because I didn't get along with my family. I also had to tell him I lost my job. It was becoming fucking complicated. He wanted to sue my company. . . .

I have been getting high a lot. We had the biggest fight ever last week when he was in town. I try not to smoke when he is in town, but I screwed up. He had one of those honey-surprises of coming home a day early. He didn't say anything about doing drugs. He thinks I'm screwing around with some other guy. The bastard put me on an allowance.

A few other women also revealed that when their significant others began suspecting they were up to something, they often thought it was infidelity rather than drug use. In other aspects, however, Sherry's story was unusual. Few women had partners like Sherry's. Others were unable to carry out such a charade.

Seldom did the women disclose their drug use voluntarily, though some admitted it when they were no longer able to hide the fact. Often, the non-using partners themselves discovered the women's crack cocaine use. Few men left the relationship immediately upon learning of their partner's drug use. More typically, they responded with disbelief and anger, followed by efforts to help their partners become drug free. The women's inability to cease using drugs was often a disappointment for both partners. Natalie, an African American woman with considerable expertise in check fraud, described how her partner left her after fourteen months.

> Dave and I both were very serious about the relationship, and we wanted it to work. I would screw up, and he actually would be supportive of me and tell me that quitting probably would take time. He understood my relapses better than I did. Every time I relapsed I felt like a nobody, like I stood him up. I got mad at him for not just kicking me out of the house, and I could not relate to him the same way I used to do. We were not equals anymore. I tried very hard, but all the shit made me nervous, and I always get high when the pressure is on. While we were going through all this, I actually started using more than before he knew about my habit.

Like Mantley and Natalie, other women described an increase in their use as they became more alienated from their partners and increasingly felt they were failing. The partners' constant checking and censoring of their behavior, along with criticism and complaints, became too much for most women.

Constant quarrels about the women's failure to give up drugs often negatively affected the couple's sex life. Several men channeled all of their energy into efforts to help their female partners give up drugs. Some women perceived themselves to be undeserving of sexual pleasures as long as they were using. One woman said, "I don't feel like I'm cheating him too much when I use as long as we don't have sex."

Other men became verbally, and sometimes physically, abusive. Their abuse often had adverse effects on the women's attitudes and self-esteem, causing them to experience heightened levels of stress as well as increased feelings of insecurity. A typical coping strategy was to increase drug use, which caused the downward spiral to accelerate. Only a few of the women who were abused reported such incidents to law enforcement officials, social service providers, or relatives. They reasoned that they deserved to be abused, they had little faith in outside intervention, and they feared that others would discover their drug use. Frequently, women with abusive experiences blamed themselves. Liz, a trained shoplifter who took pride in her skills, thought her partner's abuse was justified.

> It's all my fault. I was begging him for it. It made me feel like he wasn't perfect either. He would also feel sorry and give me a break. What he should have done is beaten the shit out of me, walked out, and closed the door behind him.

The tendency of these women to blame themselves for their partners' abuse mirrors that of non-using women in abusive relationships. Many women regretted their failure to give up drugs, a failure that almost always resulted in a broken relationship. Others, mainly those who viewed non-using men as advantageous, continued to seek partners who provided them with opportunities.

Being With a Male Drug User

The most common significant others among the women in project FAST were male crack cocaine users. Few women were involved with a partner who used drugs other than crack cocaine, although several women had been involved with such men in the past. People in general develop social relationships with persons who have similar beliefs and interests (Lazarsfeld and Merton, 1954), which helps explain the parity of the women's relationships. Drug-using partners were more sympathetic to each other's problems, led similar lives, and shared the same world view. The women frequently cited the leveling that took place in relationships when both partners used drugs. In such situations, neither partner was "better" than the other—a contrast to the situation of discordant couples in which the non-using partners often viewed themselves as superior.

As discussed earlier, steady relationships were uncommon among Older Struggling Rookies and Queens of the Scene. The Hookers and the Hustlers, regardless of their racial backgrounds, were more likely to have significant others. Initially, most women perceived such alliances as desirable. Over time, however, almost all of them faced constant pressures stemming from their own crack cocaine use and that of their partners.

Many women and their drug-using partners tended to engage only minimally in sexual activity. Despite the drug's initial disinhibiting and aphrodisiac effects, crack cocaine often damaged the long-term sexual libido of both individuals. Struggles to earn enough money to support the crack habit, the psychological effects of the drug, physical exhaustion, and the constant craving all contributed to decreased sexual activity. The association of crack cocaine use with sexual pleasure appears to be based on myth rather than reality (Macdonald et al., 1988). Nola, who shifted between hustling and hooking, for example, had been living with Pete for five years. During her interview, she suddenly realized that she and Pete had not been sexually active for a long time.

> Pete and I get along better than most couples. If you do dope,
> it is hard to stay together. The drugs tear you apart. Now, I
> would have said we used to be pretty good in bed. Not wild or
> anything, but very pleasant. I would come. He would come. He
> was having a hard time getting his little man to stand up, but
> we still made love. I didn't care for an orgasm all along. I like
> comfort, you know, like a man who holds onto you and who
> touches your body. We went from having sex to just loving and
> touching. The drugs wear you out, and you don't enjoy heavy
> sex. Two people stay together because they want to. You can
> have sex with anyone. For a short while I was hooking. Maybe
> that's when we quit doing it. I know you won't believe me, but
> I don't remember. We are pals, not lovers.

Most women were not bothered by limited sexual activity, instead receiving gratification from the shared experience of getting high. Although the growing distance between the partners seemed related to decreased sexual pleasure, the real culprit was increased crack cocaine use. Over time, the majority of the drug-using couples found themselves exclusively focused on purchasing drugs and getting high. Other researchers have described similar processes among heroin-using couples (Rosenbaum, 1981; Tucker, 1982).

Many of the single women in the study preferred to be without significant others because of previous negative experiences and exploitive relationships. From their point of view, most partners were merely a burden. Kaishinta, a single African American woman who was married once and has been engaged in two subsequent long-term relationships, described her relationships this way.

> I am one big fool. I used to always give guys a chance. That's
> because I thought I needed a man. Like, it's not about being
> married no more, but a woman should have a man. If she does
> not have one, it used to mean that something is wrong with

her. Men know this, and they mess with every lady who lets them mess around. The first guy I was with after I was divorced is the guy I still love. We were very close and connected. Our sex was great. We could sit down and shoot the breeze for hours like real partners. It all fell apart. We both were smoking crack, and that was the only thing on the mind. We'd be making love, and one of us would start talking about smoking a rock. He'd hurt me with sex if we didn't have any money for rock. You know how guys is, they take it out on the women. I got mean too, but he was too strong for me to be messing with him. He got busted, and life by myself felt pretty good. I found out how much of a pain it was to be with him or any other guy. This way, I only have to take care of myself and my own shit.

More than the white and Hispanic women in this study, African American women tended to think of their partners and relationships as a burden once they had some time to reflect by themselves. For a substantial number of women, this opportunity arose when their partners were arrested. Often, they preferred to remain single, as opposed to most of the white and Hispanic women, who more commonly moved from one relationship to the next.[1] Several African American women received more love, care, and support from relatives and friends than from the men in their lives. White and Hispanic women, however, often became alienated from their relatives and had few friends who were uninvolved with drugs.

Relationships with using partners were strained not only because of the drugs but also, in the case of the mothers, by the presence of children. According to several women, drug-using partners were less interested and willing to invest in their children than non-users. Arguments about spending money on the children were common. Many women felt that their partners underestimated their role conflicts as lovers, mothers, and often breadwinners as well. Anna, who during her own childhood ran away from home because of troubles with her stepdad, revealed tensions with her current partner over their parental responsibilities. She shouldered more responsibility than her partner.

> I'm responsible for all of it, for everything. I have to be a cute wife who always has time for her husband, a mother who loves and cares for her kids, and a booster who brings home the dough. It's too much for one person. It stresses me out, and I can't enjoy getting high. I just freak out. When I shoot up, it's like I let go of all my anger. I just found out that he wasted this week's food money on a bag. Now I'm supposed to do some extra hustling for the kids. He knows I'll do it because of the kids. I used to think a woman needs a man in the house. I'm ready to kick his ass.

The pressures associated with efforts to combine several significant social roles created a taxing situation for most of these women. Their lives, full of strain and conflict, seemed to hold no room for negotiation.

Few steady relationships between drug-using partners were successful. Drug expenses were a major point of contention in most of them. Anxiety, frustration, and sometimes anger grew as the couple encountered difficulties in supporting their drug habits. Donna, a thirty-two-year-old African American crack cocaine user for almost four years, reflected on her relationship with Ed, who also smoked crack cocaine. She resorted to prostitution to support their crack cocaine use.

> He was into rock way before me. I didn't particularly care for it. I'm more of a pot person. I also didn't like what I saw it do to him. Ed is a great guy. He never had a temper or anything. The rock makes him freeze, and once he gets out of his freeze he acts really bad. I couldn't tell you why I tried it. I was hoping it would help me understand Ed. I never smoked just rock.

I like geek joints. It kind of happened. I don't know when, but
I needed one, then two, then three or more geek joints a day. I
got totally hooked. That was our downfall. A couple that
smokes rock can't make it. You can't have a decent relationship. Like with other dope, you keep respect for yourself and
for other folks. Not with crack. When we were doing pot, we
would have a good time together. It was fun to get high. Not
with rock. He got busted three times in a row, like for disor-
derly conduct and selling rock. It's much harder for a man
than for a woman. She can sell her pussy—that's what ladies
sell. It wasn't like he asked me to do it. He didn't want me to,
but I told him I had to do it. The woman should help out. It
hurt him. He gets jealous, and he can't have sex because he
thinks about me jerking off other guys. I tell him it's different,
but he can't understand. I'm not like a geeker. I meet my guys
on the street and I only do it in their car. I try to get off the
hook, like I'll act like I'm going nuts right after he has given
me the money. That scares them.

Donna's and Ed's experience was not unusual. Crack cocaine provided a bond between them but ultimately destroyed their relationship. Many women, often Hookers,
ended up supporting two habits, their own and their partner's. A number of these women had been able to support
their own habit as Hustlers, but once they became responsible for providing their partner's drug supply, they were
forced into prostitution. Other women were pushed out of
the hustling scene because their colleagues refused to col-
laborate with them once they became involved with male
drug users who expected them to support two habits. Several male partners-in-crime of female Hustlers referred to
these men as a "disgrace." Still others were forced to leave
hustling by their male partners, who could then keep a
closer watch on their women. Other women explained that
their significant others wanted them to become prostitutes
because this accorded the men more status. Several drug-

using boyfriends of Hustlers who supported their habits found this more embarrassing than living off the earnings of a prostitute.

Not all women shifted from hustling to prostitution because of pressure from their partners. A number of women made the change because their crack habit escalated to the point where hustling became difficult. Others shifted to prostitution after being arrested several times for hustling.

Frequently, tensions in the women's relationships occurred because of a male partner's mixed feelings about the women's financial role. Beanie, whose female partner, Sandra, hustled to support both their crack habits, described his frustration.

> You have to understand that a man has his honor just like a woman does. I really care for Sandy, but she is acting as if she is wearing the pants. She's a good hustler. Man, you send her out, and she comes back with a big load of just anything. It is my job to bring it to my connection and get the money for it. I'm not sure if she is keeping some stuff for herself and turning it in for her own money, or if she is not as good at it as she used to be. She got busted. The security guards all know her. I told her she had to make enough to keep things going. I am on probation, and I don't want to be locked up again. I have been telling her that she should start selling pussy. I'll be out there with her and look out for tricks and handle the money. That way it's not just like she is bringing in the bread, but she'll be working for me.

Beanie is one of those partners who preferred that his woman be a Hooker rather than a Hustler.

The conflicts that arise when the female earns more income than the male are not unique to drug-using couples. Researchers have described similar stress among non-using working-class couples in which the women's income exceeded that of the men (Rubin, 1976). Several women reported that their male partners became abusive to compensate for their financial dependency. Dollar, who in an earlier chapter described the psychological impact of crack cocaine use, reflected on her partner's violence.

> I'm not gonna go much longer for this shit. I'm selling myself, and he's fucking acting like a pimp. I ain't taking this no more. He should be thanking me, but no, he has to show how big of a man he is. He'll be waiting for me to come back [from an act of prostitution] and sticking his hand out. I'm supposed to give him the money, and he'll buy the rock. He's acting like it's his. It's ours. Last night he came back, and he said he had to share the rock with some of his buddies. I know what he was fucking doing, showing off. That ain't right. I got mad, and he beat me up. They had to take me to the hospital. I ain't going back. I can make it by myself. He has nothing going for himself. I ain't taking this shit no more!

Women like Dollar belie traditional theories that assume that women often stay in abusive relationships because of their economic dependence on their partners. The main reasons the women in project FAST stayed in such relationships appeared to be related to their social isolation. Many felt unloved and unwanted throughout their lives. Their drug use frequently caused them to become alienated from their relatives, their childhood friends, and non-users in general. While several women began using drugs to escape their social isolation, the use of drugs, ironically, served to increase their isolation.

Lesbian Relationships

At the time of these interviews, few Hookers, Hustlers, or Queens of the Scene were involved in same-sex relationships, and all had past experiences with heterosexual relationships. Frequently, their negative experiences with men caused them to seek support from female steady partners. Although several women were involved with non-using female partners, most partners were crack cocaine users. Some women were involved with partners who used drugs other than crack cocaine and who often viewed themselves as superior to the crack users. The conflicts caused by this attitude seemed to have fewer negative consequences for the relationship than the similar conflicts of heterosexual couples. Gabe, who had been living with her female partner for four years following a six-year marriage to a male user, summarized the differences in her relationships.

> We get high, and we already know that we'll start arguing and fighting with each other. But things are different. It's hard to say. It's not like one of us is always the one hustling money or that one of us tells the other what to do. It all works naturally. We don't talk about it. A man is a pain. They sweet talk you, and you're supposed to sell your body because that's what women do. Me and my partner try to get by without tricking, but we'll do it if we have to. We tell each other about it. You couldn't do that with a guy.
>
> We still make love, and it's great. It's not about coming. It's about enjoying it, and being close. I guess the big difference for me is that I don't feel pressured by a guy. I feel like I can make my own decisions. She smokes pot and snorts cocaine. Sometimes she puts me down because I smoke crack cocaine. That bothers me. How can she believe in all those stereotypes?

The dynamics in the user/non-user relationships between two women differed from those in the mixed-gender couples. According to the women, same-sex partners treated them with more respect even though they also wanted them to stop using crack. Yvette, a twenty-one-year-old Hispanic Hustler, discussed the dynamics in her relationship.

> We go at it all the time, but in a decent way. None of this macho stuff of putting the other person down and making her

feel bad. We argue, and we disagree, but we also respect each other. She sees me as a person who uses drugs, not as a drug user only. I used to not be able to relate to that. I have been beaten up and kicked out in the cold before by a very decent-acting guy who lost it with me. Now that I smoke crack, things have gotten worse. I used to rip her off, sold her stereo and everything. I knew she would kick me out, but she didn't. She was mad as hell, but she was also there to help me. She doesn't want me to get wasted. I sure hope it'll stay like this because I have a long way to go.

The lack of gender conflicts provided more potential for same-sex relationships to succeed as compared to hetero-sexual relationships. Reports of physical abuse were rare. Nevertheless, most couples in which both women used crack cocaine also seemed to focus more on drugs than on love.

Several Hookers in same-sex relationships added that they preferred to have a female significant other because having sex with men was how they earned their living. Cari, who in the introduction referred to the independence of African American women, explained her preference for women as steady partners.

Tricking is a job. To be good at it, you keep your emotions out of it. You have to be professional. It's hard to be with one guy and think about him as a client and to go home and be with another guy, doing the same thing, and telling yourself this is love. Being with a lady is what I prefer. It doesn't get things messed up as much.

Although the women involved in same-sex relationships in project FAST were familiar with the concept of lesbian-ism, a majority of them did not identify themselves as les-bians. They assumed that being lesbian was an ideology. As one woman put it, "I'm not like a dyke. That's a political thing." Lewis (1979) described similar assumptions among older women, who became involved in lesbian relationships after heterosexual experiences. For most of these women, the involvement in same-sex relationships occurred coincidentally, without their making a clear choice to become lesbians. Most of those who were involved in same-sex relationships did not want the additional stigma of "lesbianism" added to the stigma they already carried as drug users.

Adult Role Models

Half of the women in project FAST were raised by two biological parents; in one-third of these cases, the parents were legally married. Another third of the study participants, mainly African American women, grew up in female single-parent households. The social and economic circumstances of their families greatly affected the women's perspectives on intimate relationships. Several women accepted their mothers' perceptions of men's unwillingness to commit to a relationship and they believed they would be happier as single women. Others wanted to prove their mothers incorrect.

Those raised in households in which an adult had an alcohol or drug problem recalled that this experience placed a strain not only on the adult relationship but also on the children. Laura, a Hispanic Hooker, remembered a very difficult childhood.

> I know I always want to stay single. No man in my house. That way he won't be in my way, and I won't be in his. My dad always was an alcoholic, and he spent our food money on drinks and stuff. He'd come home and be angry with himself, us, and the world. I understand that he felt powerless. Like when he was laid off his job. He just threw the furniture through the house, broke all the dishes, and hit all of us. My mom started drinking, too, and I ran away because two drunks just was too much for me.

Laura's story is typical, and many women like her who saw the suffering of one or both parents vowed to remain single but ended up in similar relationships nevertheless. Foxtrot, one of the African American Hookers, described a repetitive cycle of drug use and exploitive relationships.

> My mom tried to take care of us, but I guess we didn't get there. Two of my brothers passed from AIDS. One of them got shot, though. She tried hard to raise us, but she always had a lot of shit going on in her life. Guys would move in and out, and there always was some kind of problem. None of them ever had a decent job. They'd be drunks or addicts. At first, she'd be getting drunk too and next thing we find out, she's shooting dope. I ain't doing much better. Seems like I never learned how to do it right with a man.

Other women were raised in households in which the adult caregivers were in healthy relationships. Frequently, these women had higher expectations of their own relationships, although they realized their crack cocaine use served as a major barrier. Their lifestyle also offered them few opportunities to meet men who could be supportive. In general, most women in this study were skeptical about the possibility of being involved in long-term, positive relationships.

Ideal Relationships

Many women dreamed about "meeting their prince on the white horse and being happily married forever after." Sue, a white Hooker who was already working as a street prostitute before becoming involved with crack cocaine, contrasted her own experience with that of her parents.

> My parents are cool, and they still love each other. They'll have a fight, but before you know it, they are kissing and hugging again. I'll never have something like that. Even if I would

quit using, I still have a bad reputation, and no man would want me after all the things I have done. I'm not a crack head, but I have been busted and that kind of stuff. But you never know. You asked me about five years from now, and I can see myself with a nice house, a car, a husband, kids, and a dog, just like you see on TV. I still have hope, but I know that it probably won't happen to me in this lifetime.

Women raised in middle-class households frequently were more cynical about the link between happiness and socio-economic status. For them, owning property and having access to luxuries often concealed other troubles. At the same time, however, they realized that economic means could provide independence. Several Queens of the Scene and some Hustlers explained that their level of income allowed them to survive without a steady relationship. They preferred casual relationships for temporary emotional support and sex. For most women in this study, their wishes about ideal relationships revealed a dualism of romanticism and pragmatism. The latter often included drugs, sex, and companionship.

When the women were asked to define an ideal relationship, few were able to respond immediately. They emphasized needing to know themselves better before they could provide an answer. Others did not believe in ideal relationships and based their position on previous negative experiences. Frequently, they showed a level of resistance that kept them from hypothetically considering a happy, long-term alliance. As Teranda, a mother of three, said:

I like it by myself. No other people to worry about. When the kids were younger, I thought it would be nice to have someone around . . . I tried. I didn't think much about it. A woman is told that she should have a man around the house. If you can't find Mr. Right, you take Mr. Second or Third. I have been stood up too many times. I don't know if it's me or the guys. I expect a lot from a man, like his family is number one, being honest, having a job, and respecting himself, talking with me, and those kind of little touches. Men want a woman but no responsibility. For me, being by myself makes life easier. Women have to learn that they don't have to be with a man in order to be happy.

Some women had been involved in ideal or close-to-ideal relationships in the past. These relationships failed either because of the woman's drug use while in a relationship with a non-user or because of the male partner's failure to accept and care for the women's children. They continually had to renegotiate their social roles as partner and as mother. In their eyes, an ideal relationship should not force them to choose between their partner and their children. Women who entered relationships based on romantic feelings stressed the need for romance in ideal relationships. However, they tended to have more past failed relationships than women who acknowledged practical reasons for entering and maintaining relationships. Several women indicated that an ideal relationship implied no drug use. They agreed that an ideal relationship, or any positive relationship for that matter, would be impossible if one or both partners used drugs. They reiterated that in most cases drug use will dominate the relationship, causing the partners to focus on the shared drug-use role while ignoring other social roles. At the same time, however, they continued to use drugs and often blamed external circumstances for their negative experiences.

The ideal situations described by many of the women shared the following components: reciprocal caring, nurturing, communicating, understanding, and forgiving. They acknowledged that their own drug use often caused them to be less loyal, sincere, trustworthy, and respectful. Melinda, who feared embarrassing herself when she began smoking marijuana, offered her vision of an ideal relationship.

> It can only be for real if two people want it, if two people love each other. It needs to be something you and your partner feel. It's no good if you have to tell yourself you have to care for the other person. It needs to come natural, and it will if the relationship is good. Two people should talk and listen, and if one person makes a mistake, the other person needs to be willing to forgive. That doesn't mean you should let the other person walk over you, but if the relationship is good, that won't happen. Too often, people use another person's mistake to get something from that person. That is disrespect. You need loving, caring, and sharing, no matter what. But it needs to come from two people.

Very few women in project FAST mentioned sexuality as an aspect of an ideal relationship, which supports the belief that sexuality is not directly linked to romanticism. Many women viewed sexual activity as a component of their relationships and as a survival strategy. Sex was at the core of the relationship for only a few women.

4 Reproduction and Motherhood

Drug use posed major challenges to the women in project FAST, especially regarding their reproductive choices. Most of their pregnancies were unplanned, sometimes even unwanted, and created dilemmas regarding their reproductive options. Several women's crack cocaine use harmed the fetus before they were even aware of the pregnancy. Many wondered whether to continue the pregnancy or to seek an abortion. They contemplated becoming mothers or giving the child up for adoption. Those few women who planned their pregnancies sometimes were trying to compensate for a child that was taken away by legal authorities or to seek what they saw as the "healing" effects of a pregnancy. Others planned pregnancies hoping to motivate partners to remain in relationships with them. Some hoped the pregnancy would provide them with someone to love and care for. A few younger women saw pregnancy as a way to start their own households. Until recently, when welfare policies were reformed, young mothers and their offspring were eligible for welfare assistance, including subsidized housing.

Several women intentionally remained childless, believing themselves to be unprepared for motherhood because they used drugs, had limited financial resources, or lived below subsistence conditions. Few Queens of the Scene had children, not only because they tended to be young but also because their jobs were not compatible with motherhood. Several Queens of the Scene were told by their employers that they would lose their jobs if they became pregnant.

Little research has been done on the difficulties of reproductive decision-making and the meaning of motherhood to female drug users (Kearney, Murphy, and Rosenbaum, 1994). Typically, investigators have limited their focus to the impact of women's drug use on the development of the unborn fetus and the relationship between mothers and newborns (Rosenbaum, 1981; Chasnoff, 1986; Deren, 1986; Taylor, 1993). The perspectives of the women themselves—their attitudes, values, norms, interpretations, and decision-making processes—are seldom considered.

Contraceptive Use

All of the women in this study had at least heard of family and reproductive planning and the majority had used one or more contraceptive during their lives. Male condoms were the most frequently used form of contraception, followed by birth control pills. The use of an IUD, sponge, or other contraceptive was less common. Only a few of the women had tried the female condom, describing it as the most demeaning method of contraception, difficult to use, and uncomfortable.

A substantial number of women believed that drugs served as contraceptives, making it difficult if not impossible for them to conceive. Despite their knowledge about protection and their familiarity with female drug users who did conceive, the belief that drug use prevented pregnancies remained popular. One woman called this phenomenon the "cop-out myth," explaining that as long as women thought drugs served as a contraceptive, they did not have to take steps to prevent conception. "If a woman like that becomes pregnant, she'll never say she could have done something about it," this woman said. "No, she'll say it's a miracle. Like, you know, with Mary and Jesus."

Despite their actions, the women in this study frequently affirmed that contraceptives gave them a sense of control, allowing them to make decisions about reproduction and to be sexually active. However, the most commonly used method, the condom, provided them with little actual control because their male partners, not they themselves, had to wear the condom. Amaro (1995) has described how this discrepancy creates gendered power differences and makes the woman the vulnerable party.

Sex with casual partners more typically involved condom use than sex with steady partners. Tarintha, an African American woman who traded sex for money on the stroll but also exchanged sex for crack in one of the nearby crack houses, explained:

> How am I supposed to answer your question about telling the guy I am with to use a rubber? I'd never think about bringing it up with Mike [her steady partner]. He'd knock me off the bed. With my tricks, they know it is part of the business. You buy a pussy, but you ain't just putting it in. I'm serious. If they don't like it, they can find someone else. Now, over at the houses it is different. You don't have the tricks, but you have guys who get high and sell rocks. Some of them want to be laid. I pretty much know how much I can smoke with my money, but it does happen that I want more. I may go find myself a trick and come back. If I need a rock badly, I do it with one of the guys in the house. You kinda have to play the condom thing by ear. If I'm really down, and I want a hit very badly, I'll just do it. Listen, if I can help it, I pull out a rubber, and I make them think it is special. They know I am a hooker and that I can make a guy feel more with a rubber than with-

out. Okay, that's what they want to believe. Guys have this
fantasy sex thing about hookers.

Female prostitutes have confirmed similar differences in
condom use by type of partner (Sterk, 1990). Most of these
women considered it difficult, and often inappropriate, to
propose condom use to their steady partners. Often they
feared that these significant others would view the request
as a sign of distrust, an insinuation of promiscuity on the
men's part, which was in fact the case. Others were afraid
that asking their steady partners to use condoms would be
a violation of gender-role expectations. Requiring that casual partners use condoms was less problematic because of
their limited emotional involvement with these men. Paying clients, however, often wanted to be in charge and re-
sented being told what to do. As one prostitution customer
reported:

I pick up chicks all the time. You don't want to date a chick,
but you want to have sex with her. If it's a serious relationship,
you have to listen to each other and respect what the other
person wants. If it's just about sex, a man can tell the woman
what to do. If she don't like it, she shouldn't let him pick
her up.

Not only did paying partners become upset when women
suggested condom use, steady and non-paying partners became agitated as well. Sometimes they threatened violence
if the women refused to have unprotected sex. In chapter 7
the violent encounters and abuse these women faced will
be discussed in more detail. In addition, condom use as a
risk-reduction strategy for HIV infection is a central focus of
chapter 6.

The extent of condom use also varied by the social context in which the sexual activity occurred. Queens of the
Scene coerced into sex by their employers never proposed

condom use. Similarly, most Older Struggling Rookies believed that they lacked the control or power to suggest that their partners use condoms. In addition, several women felt uncomfortable even touching a condom. Among the Hookers and the Hustlers, the presence of drugs often affected their intentions and actual requests for protected sex. Condom use was least likely when both partners were high on drugs. In several cases, the craving for drugs overrode these women's intention to ask partners to use condoms. Overall, the Hookers, especially those who worked as prostitutes prior to using crack cocaine, felt most comfortable proposing condom use.

Condom use varied by type of sexual activity. Few women proposed condom use when performing fellatio. The men frequently complained that the condoms reduced their sexual excitement. In addition, the women often disliked the taste of condoms, despite the marketing of condoms with flavors such as peppermint and banana. A number of women pointed out that men often take more time to ejaculate when a condom is used in oral sex. While this did not frustrate them when having oral sex with significant others, it became a major deterrent with casual partners, especially paying ones.

Condom use during vaginal intercourse was more common, although few women reported using condoms consistently. Factors contributing to inconsistent use included being high on drugs, craving drugs, resistance on the part of partners or the women themselves, and lack of availability. Tina, an African American Hooker, shared her view of men, sex, and condoms.

> It's tough. I like condoms. For one thing, a condom can keep dirt and diseases away. You never know who has been with whom. Nobody's gonna tell you the truth about that anyway.

The lubrication makes it slide in easy, and a woman can have more sex without getting dry. But if a woman doesn't douche behind it, it can give her a terrible irritation. I know that from my own experience. I'm one of those women who likes the guy to wear a rain coat [condom] all the time, but then I won't walk away if the guy wants to do it without, or if we can't get a rubber. Like, I might run out of rubbers. The guys almost never have one on them. That should tell you something about how they feel about using rubbers. Them bastards don't care. They ain't the ones getting sick and pregnant. The guys around here sweet talk you like you can't believe it. No guy will tell you he has a disease, even if his thing is about to fall off. I have been beaten up for wanting to use a condom. It happens all over the place. Women get fucked over. Hey, I ain't begging a guy to put a rubber on. I don't ask anymore. I know that's like an excuse. I can't read his mind. I say they don't want to use one, but I never ask.

Many women were upset that they were expected to provide condoms for their male partners. In general, they held mixed attitudes and beliefs regarding condom use.

Accurate information about the extent of condom use is difficult to collect. In this study, for example, the number of women who reported that their partners used a condom most of the time was much higher than the number who reported condom use during their last sexual encounter. One woman acknowledged that she had exaggerated condom use among her partners.

I thought you was one of them health department people, like a condom preacher. I have enough folks breathing down my neck. I didn't need you telling me I was screwing up. So, I gave you the "right" answer.

The birth control pill was the second most commonly used contraceptive, but many women had complaints about it. The most common of these were the pill's association with medication, the necessity of regular use, and rumors about its causing infertility.

> I ain't taking medication, like I have some type of disease. It gives me the bee hives.
>
> My body should be able to tell me when to get my period and not some pills from the doctor. It's also hard to take it every day, and I would only take it when I happen to think about taking it. One time, I took a whole bunch of pills, thinking it might help me get high.
>
> The pill made me gain weight, and I got depressed. I have heard that if you take the pill too long, you can't get kids no more.

By contrast, a frequently cited advantage was that the birth control pill required no negotiation with sex partners. The decision remained totally in the women's hands. For those women who had no health insurance, which was a substantial number in this study, the expense of birth control pills was too much at times or led to quarrels with steady partners.

Pregnancy

On average, the women in this study reported three pregnancies. Only a few had never been pregnant, and one woman had been pregnant eight times. Because most of their pregnancies were unplanned, many women recalled being shocked and panicked when they found out they were pregnant. For some women, this moment did not occur until they were in their second or third trimester. As other researchers have noted, female drug users tend to have irregular menstrual cycles (Rosenbaum, 1981; Deren, 1986), which causes them to be less aware of potential pregnancies.

Not only were most pregnancies unplanned, the women's sexual activity was often unplanned as well. Stacy, a twenty-five-year-old white Hustler with two young children, talked about drugs, sex, and reproduction.

> Becoming a mom is a big deal. It's what makes women different from men. It gives women the job to make sure there's a next generation. It also shows that a woman is for real. I never had anybody to explain to me how it all works but you kind of find out. I mean, you talk with your friends about it, you read about it, and you try. Some days you take more chances than others. It's a woman's job to protect herself. I know all about that. I just don't want to think about that crap every time I do it. How can you enjoy it if you have to worry about getting pregnant? You get carried away even more when drugs are involved. When a guy sticks his thing in you, you don't think about a big tummy and a baby. I don't know if you would call it an accident or not. There isn't much time to think about it. Anyway, the pregnancy thing makes it hard for women. It's a good thing that the drugs make it hard for a woman to become pregnant.

Many women learned they were pregnant when they went to the doctor for some other reason. Others received a pregnancy test upon admittance to a drug treatment center or prison. In many cases, they had already been pregnant for several weeks or months by the time they learned about their condition. Debra, who hustled to support her habit, was one of them. She did not know she was pregnant until she was told she would deliver within ten weeks, and said that she would have stopped using drugs had she known.

> When you are getting high, everything makes sense because nothing makes sense. I mean, every woman knows that if she's not having her period, something is up. It took me a while to figure out I hadn't had my period for a long time. I had these tampons over at the house, and one day I said, "Damn, I haven't used one of those babies for a long time." But that was

it. I got busted, and I was trying to get some extra attention.
I told the nurse that I was sick to my stomach, and I started
throwing up. It was a con game. This lady took a test, and I
find out I am fucking pregnant. I don't know when it happened. The doctor told me, it must have been a while ago. The
baby'll be here in like ten weeks. I guess they can tell from
the TV screen. I mean, I wouldn't have been getting high if I'd
known.

Other women reduced or otherwise changed their drug
intake once they learned about their pregnancy. A number
of them shifted from using crack cocaine, an illegal substance, to drinking alcohol, which, because it is legal, many
women believed to be safer. Others began using marijuana
or heroin, drugs with a mellowing effect, because they believed them to be safer for the fetus than the harsher effects
of crack cocaine.

The women believed it inappropriate to continue to use
crack cocaine once they were aware of their pregnancy. One
woman said, "A pregnant woman would not mess with
drugs because every time she gets high, she could be hurt-
ing or killing the baby." According to another woman, "Using drugs as a pregnant woman is the wrong thing to do.
The fetus does not ask to get high or to be born as an addict." Several women, however, were unable to change
their drug intake despite knowing they were pregnant, as
discussed later in this chapter.

A number of women refused to seek prenatal care and
delivered their babies without the assistance of the medical
system. Some delivered at home, sometimes with the help
of a lay midwife from the community. Others delivered
without any professional help, at times in drug-use settings.
Verna, a white woman who delivered her second child in a
crack house, said:

I want to be a good mom for this one. They took my other
baby when she was a few months old. Someone from the
neighborhood called, and the cops or somebody found out that
I was smoking way too much [crack]. I think that the social
work lady felt sorry for me, maybe being a woman herself. I'm
gonna keep this one, believe you me. No one is taking this
little boy. He is adorable. I make him sleep and eat as much as
he needs to, and I will never spend anything on drugs if I need
it for him. He has nice clothes, too. I cut down on the crack.
The last time I smoked a lot was right before I delivered my
baby. I knew he was about to come, and I had heard that it's
easier if you smoke. It makes you get contractions or something. I delivered in the bathroom. People were freaking out.
A woman from the neighborhood came out and helped. She
was very angry with me, but she also understood that I
couldn't give up another baby.

Penny, a drug user who was pregnant for the first time,
also feared losing custody of her soon-to-be-born child.
Like many other female drug users, she had struggled to
quit using drugs. In her own words:

I'm plenty pregnant, and you can see I got something coming.
I look forward to being a mommy. I love children, and I think
I'll be good at it. I am a very patient type. I want this baby so
much, I can't tell you. I am already attached to it, like I feel it
all the time. I get very nervous when I don't feel anything. I'm
trying to smoke less and really, I should quit. I wish there was
any way I could get away from drugs and the neighborhood.
Being around it all the time makes it tough. If I just could not
smoke for a few days, I could go see a doctor. If I can't quit and
the baby has something wrong with it, I don't know what I'll
do with myself.

The women's fear of criminalization and loss of custody
grew in the early 1990s as the political climate became more
supportive of the prosecution and incarceration of pregnant

drug users and less concerned with providing them with drug treatment (Maher, 1990; Roberts, 1991). A number of women were aware of local policies requiring social and health service providers to report pregnant drug users to the legal authorities (Lieb and Sterk-Elifson, 1995).[1]

In the crack cocaine scene, little support existed to assist pregnant women to reduce or stop using the drug. Most drug dealers continued to sell to a woman even when they knew of her pregnancy. Female dealers, including the Queens of the Scene, tended to be more critical of their pregnant customers than their male counterparts were. Sharon, one of the Queens of the Scene in charge of four street dealers, explained:

> I don't do much of any drug myself. I mainly snort coke, and I might freebase some when I'm partying. You can't be in the business and get high all the time. For sure not if you are a woman. Everybody will try to screw you over. I know what drugs can do to people. I have seen plenty of addicts. Drugs take over the mind and soul. I never have any of my people sell to pregnant ladies, and if they do, I better not find out. The women get pissed with me, but later they come and say, "Thank you, you are the most decent person I know." If a woman is having a very hard time, I tell her to snort a few lines, but not to smoke. With heroin it is different, because you get damned sick when you quit. It takes more time to get your habit down.

Dealers like Sharon, however, were exceptions. Typically, other drug users failed to provide support to the women while they were pregnant. Several Hookers had been forced to reduce their drug intake. Their pregnancy led to a decrease in their income as fewer men were attracted to having sex with a pregnant prostitute. Among the Hustlers, on the other hand, a number of pregnant women increased their earnings from shoplifting by taking advantage of their maternity clothes. As one woman said, "Those clothes give you a lot of room to hide things."

Abortions and Miscarriages

Abortions were not uncommon among the women in this study, and a substantial number of women reported having sought one. Several women considered an abortion but failed to get one, either because they had already reached the second trimester of the pregnancy, lacked the financial means, or did not know where to go. Some women indicated that they had contemplated an abortion but decided against it for religious reasons. Abortion was as controversial an issue among the women in project FAST as it is in society at large. Most women were ambivalent about abortion and those who did abort a pregnancy often felt guilty about their decision.

The most common reason for an abortion was that the women, and sometimes their partners, felt unable to provide for a child. One woman remarked:

> I don't need no baby no more. I can't even take care of myself with my drug habit. On top of everything, me and my boyfriend ain't getting along. I don't need no baby by myself, that's for sure.

Another woman said:

> Me and my partner felt that if we ever were gonna make it, we should not have a child to worry about. He went with me to the clinic. I think he was afraid I would change my mind. I still feel guilty about it. I felt guilty even as we walked into the clinic. He just didn't understand, and he called me all sorts of

names. We broke up about this whole thing. I would cry and cry and cry. He just couldn't understand how I could love something that didn't even exist.

Eight women chose an abortion because of the circumstances in which they conceived. Five of them became pregnant in a prostitution encounter, and the other three were impregnated by a rapist. Few women aborted because of the potential damage already done to the fetus as a result of their crack cocaine use.

Only a small number of women involved the potential father in their decision to have an abortion, either because they did not know who fathered the child or because they feared the father's disapproval of their decision. In general, they tended not to discuss their decision with anybody, including their closest friends, because of the stigma often attached to abortion.

Initially, many women described their decision to abort as a rational decision that was easy to make. Subsequent comments, however, indicated that they agonized over feelings of guilt and constant doubts.

Miscarriages were viewed as another form of pregnancy termination. Almost half of the women in project FAST reported a miscarriage, and half of these believed that the miscarriage resulted from their crack cocaine use. Some women intentionally smoked excessive amounts of crack cocaine, hoping this would cause them to miscarry. They perceived crack-induced miscarriages as less negative and stigmatizing than abortions. Other women, however, claimed that such "intentional" miscarriages were equivalent to an abortion and made no distinction between the two. Among the women who opposed abortion, the crack-induced miscarriages were more acceptable than an abortion. One woman, who did miscarry and attributed it to her excessive crack cocaine use, said:

> If you have a miscarriage, it kinda means you couldn't help it. Nature made the decision for you. If it is an abortion, the woman herself decided she didn't want the baby. Everybody knows that smoking lots of rock makes a baby go away. In the newspaper they call that murder, but as far as I am concerned, it is not. For one thing, you never know for sure if it will work with rock. For another thing, I know several women who have done it, and they are nice people. They knew they couldn't care for the kid. Also, a miscarriage makes people feel sorry for you, and that can carry you a long way.

The main cause of miscarriages unrelated to drugs was physical abuse, most frequently by a male partner or by other drug users. Angel, a white Hooker, was impregnated by a man other than her steady partner. She recalled her miscarriage.

> I can't tell you how special it was to be pregnant. I never much thought about it, but it was like a gift from God when they told me I was expecting a baby. It was hard on Pete [her steady partner] because he had just come out of prison. He knew I was supporting myself by walking the street. He got me hooked, and I never had to worry about having drugs. Once they locked him up, some of his buddies took care of me but they wanted favors . . . yeah, sex. I figured, I may as well become a whore and decide for myself who I'll do it with. Knowing that the baby wasn't his made him angry. We talked about it, but he said he loved me so much, he'd stay with me and be the baby's father. Something got into him. I walked into the house, and he was like all upset, and I could tell he had been getting high. I walked up the stairs, and I remember that he kicked me in the stomach. I rolled down the stairs and woke up in the hospital. I lost the baby.

While the women described both abortion and miscarriage as very traumatic, the trauma was most severe for women like Angel, whose pregnancy was terminated by a violent act.

Reproductive Choices and Changes in Drug-Use Patterns

Once they realized that they were pregnant, most women were forced to face the potential consequences of their continued crack cocaine use. To some extent, their reproductive decision-making overlapped with decisions regarding their drug use. In addition, the reproductive choices of some women were affected by their feelings for the man who fathered the child. Women who became pregnant by a steady partner often continued their pregnancies. As one woman said, "At least I know the child comes from a man I liked." Although none of the women in this study was able to cease using drugs, many did try, sometimes successfully, to cut down on their drug use when they were pregnant. The few women who quit using drugs during their pregnancy, however, began using again soon after delivery.

Some women decided while pregnant to give the child up for adoption. The drug use of these women tended to be erratic, reflecting to some degree their emotions about the decision. For example, their drug intake tended to increase when they felt like failures and to decrease when they realized that even though they would not be the main caretaker, they wanted the child to be healthy at birth. One woman stressed that if her child was unhealthy, it would be impossible to find someone to adopt the baby. Pregnancies due to sexual encounters with casual partners often yielded a decision to terminate the pregnancy. Those women who sought intentionally to miscarry often increased their drug use. The drug-use patterns among women who decided to terminate their pregnancy tended to remain constant.

Motherhood

The women in this study were no different from women in general in placing a high value on motherhood.[2] When asked about the most important aspects of their lives, many women told stories of their children, some, especially the Older Struggling Rookies, about their grandchildren. They talked about the ups and downs in the children's lives, about their struggles as mothers who are crack cocaine users, and about having lost custody. At the same time, they described the joys of motherhood, the accomplishments of their children, and their expectations for their children's future. A central theme involved the ongoing conflict between their roles as mothers and as drug users. On the one hand, most women experienced difficulties controlling their crack cocaine use, while on the other they sought to demonstrate that they were worthy mothers. They associated this worthiness with acting responsibly, providing material and emotional support, and being available to their child or children. Several women indicated that they also gained something from their role as mothers. Those with young children enjoyed the unconditional love they received. Valerie, who began experimenting with drugs when her mother worked evening and night shifts, said:

> A good mother loves her child more than anything else. She should be willing to give up everything else in her life. I want to love my baby girl, and I do my best to love her, nurture her, and be close. I love to fix her hair and dress her up like a little doll. I know that I am doing my job because she loves me back. She smiles at me, and she wants to hug me when she sees me. She wants me to stay with her, and she cries every time I leave.

It seemed that some women compensated for their social isolation by closely attaching themselves to their children.

Liz, who was abused as both a child and an adult, described the importance of love between mothers and their children.

> My boy should have a much better life than I had. My mama was always gone. When she was home, she would be sleeping. She never took time for me and my brother. She's like a stranger. Like, she didn't notice that me and my brother was on drugs. It took for my brother to have to go to jail for her to find out. She would buy things for us and leave us money, but there was never no love. I want to love my boy, listen to him tell me stories, watch him, play with him, and make him feel worthwhile.

Despite Liz's intentions, she spent much of her time hustling money for her crack habit, but also to buy presents for her son. Several other women mentioned similar struggles.

Researchers studying crack cocaine use among mothers in the San Francisco Bay area (Kearney, Murphy, and Rosenbaum, 1994), have also reported a clash between the social roles of being a mother and being a drug user. They found that crack cocaine use limited the women's success in their maternal roles. On the other hand, however, many women in their study used "defensive compensation" to be good mothers despite their drug use. Like the San Francisco women, the women in project FAST constantly sought strategies by which to integrate these conflicting social roles. For example, some women used drugs only out of view of their children and during times that it would least affect the children, such as when they were asleep or in school. Others always made sure they bought groceries and other necessities before spending money on drugs. Several Hookers and Hustlers worked overtime to provide for their children. However, their income-generating activities forced them to spend more time outside the home and away from their children. Anita Garey (1995) described how nurses who worked the night shift also experienced difficulty with their roles as mothers. In addition, the involvement in illegal activities among the project FAST women often led to their arrest, which took them away from their children for longer periods of time. The women's entrance into drug treatment, which could be voluntary or court-ordered, created a similar loss of contact.

Few women directly acknowledged the large extent to which their crack cocaine use interfered with their role as mothers. Gloria, a mother of two daughters who supported her family with income from her prostitution activities, described the impact of her use.

> Crack is no drug. It is dangerous poison. It takes over your mind, and I catch myself selling everything. Like my own body or diapers for the baby. Every bloodsucker who has rock can get me. Crack makes you think about nothing else than getting high. I keep on hoping to get a good rush, but it only makes me jittery and aggressive. I fucking forget my kids. I have sent them out of the house in cold and rainy weather because I didn't want them to see that people were getting high in the apartment and screwing each other. I have also locked them in the bedroom, and I would forget about them. I would hear them cry, but it didn't mean anything. I am a good mother. . . . When I'm not smoking, I tell myself, "never again." I play with them, we buy groceries together, and we eat. I'm a good mom as long as I can keep my hands away from the next rock.

Among the Older Struggling Rookies, most women had already raised their children prior to their involvement with crack cocaine. Several of them believed it would have been impossible to take care of their children if they had been using crack at the time.

A number of women believed that the mother's role varies with the children's age. Infants and babies, for example, are completely dependent and require round-the-clock care. But they also sleep long hours, allowing time for their mothers to get high. Once their children got older, several mothers feared being found out. Lathia, a Hustler who aspired to become a dealer, had a five-year-old girl.

> Jenny just turned five and she is a smart girl. I used to be able to get high in the house and she wouldn't know what was going on. Now, she knows what is happening. What if she tells the wrong folks? When I get high and she is in the house, I can't even enjoy it. Maybe that's a good thing. She might be my savior angel.

The mothers of older children, particularly adolescents, reported difficulty in disciplining them. Frequently, their children criticized their mothers and lacked respect for them as parents. As one fourteen-year-old said, "Why should I listen to an addict? She can't even get her own life together."

A few women in this study asked older children to take care of their younger siblings, but in most cases they were unable to substitute for the mothers. Others asked relatives to care for their children. The African American women in project FAST were most likely to have support from relatives, a fact supported by other research (Minkler and Roe, 1993; Rosenbaum, 1981; Stack, 1974). Several women arranged informal adoptions, or temporary family arrangements to prevent formal adoption or loss of legal custody.

Some of these women rationalized that even many non-using mothers failed in their mothering role, and that crack cocaine use was not necessarily at fault. Some believed that drug use might actually even help some women cope with the challenges of motherhood, a finding also corroborated by others (Rosenbaum, 1981; Taylor, 1993). Some women compared themselves with mothers, often middle-class women, who used prescription drugs or alcohol.

A number of the Older Struggling Rookies were taking care of their grandchildren, frequently because their daughters were drug users. Now that they had become users themselves, however, they were less able to fulfill that responsibility. The non-using daughter of one of the Older Struggling Rookies asked her mother to assist with the rearing of her grandchildren. She hoped this responsibility would motivate her mother to stop using crack cocaine.

Several women lost custody of one or more of their children because of their crack cocaine use. Typically, this experience was painful, and some women equated it with their failure as mothers and as women. Some women compensated for the loss of one child by having another, even while they continued to use drugs. Overall, the women's views on motherhood were paradoxical. They wanted to be mothers, but they also wanted to use drugs. They claimed to be good mothers, but they also acknowledged their failures in this role.

5 Off and On

EXPERIENCES WITH DRUG TREATMENT

At the time of their participation in the study, none of the women in project FAST was in drug treatment.[1] However, many had previous treatment experiences, some in every city where they had lived. The Older Struggling Rookies were an exception; none of them ever had been in drug treatment or even considered it. These older, relatively recent initiates to crack cocaine commonly believed that they could quit drugs without professional help. Some considered drug treatment an embarrassment because it would show their lack of self-control.

Two of the Queens of the Scene had had previous drug treatment experiences. Angy, one of the dealers, had recently entered an inpatient program because she feared her jealous boss might abuse her. She dropped out of the program, however, as soon as she learned that another main dealer wanted to hire her. The other woman had been in treatment as an adolescent, and none of her affiliates knew about this part of her past. Queens of the Scene generally agreed that a person who slipped, or lost control over a drug habit, should be barred from operating in the higher echelons of the drug business.

Two-thirds of the Hustlers and the Hookers had been in drug treatment, primarily in publicly-funded programs. Their stories reflected their experiences and their assessment of the advantages and disadvantages of inpatient and

119

outpatient treatment programs. They often complained that unlike heroin, where methadone can be used to treat addiction, there was no substitute for crack cocaine.[2] Women who used heroin also tended to have used methadone. Marta, a white Hustler whose drug-use history included heroin injection prior to crack cocaine, articulated the following:

> Heroin still is my drug. I love it, and if it wasn't for the dope dealer, I'd still be using it. The dealers got all screwed up because they could make more money with the ready rock. There used to be good heroin all over town, now there's maybe four places in town where you can buy heroin. I mean, they call it heroin, but it is shit. I'm telling you, you take it, but most of the time you don't feel shit. They must've cut it at least fifteen times. I got myself into the methadone program and I was getting more high off my methadone than off the heroin. They liked me in the program, and they'd throw away my dirty piss [positive urine screen]. I don't particularly care for ready rock, but a person has to have something. I use the methadone with the crack and it's a sweet high.

As high-quality heroin and powdered cocaine became less available on the local drug market, women who injected heroin and/or cocaine often felt forced to shift to smoking crack cocaine, which was readily available. Several women, regardless of whether they had used heroin in the past, began using heroin to qualify for methadone maintenance treatment. Zena, a twenty-seven-year-old Puerto Rican Hooker who injected cocaine, had been in outpatient programs in New York City and Washington, D.C. before she moved to Atlanta. Together with a friend, she turned to heroin to gain access to methadone. They preferred methadone over alcohol and marijuana to cope with the crash that follows a crack cocaine high.

This one guy started selling methadone. I'd heard that methadone was great to get the monkey off your back. I watched
people use it, and it made them peaceful, like more than
smoking blunt [marijuana in a cigar]. They have to find heroin
in your system to get into the methadone program. Me and
this other girl bought some, and we used it for about five days.
We'd make sure we had some of them needle tracks. We made
it into the clinic. It's great because the high is good, and it's
cheaper than buying reefer.

Entering maintenance treatment programs to gain access to methadone instead of buying marijuana to soften
the crash from a crack cocaine high was a recent phenomenon among the women in this study. For women like Zena,
the decision to enter drug treatment was made for pragmatic reasons.

Many other women saw their drug treatment efforts as a
sign of their commitment to get off drugs. In reality, however, external circumstances often forced them to enter
drug treatment. Those women who had experiences with
drug treatment presented a wide range of reasons for entering such programs. These reasons, the barriers they encountered, and their actual treatment experiences form the
core of this chapter.

Motivators for Seeking Drug Treatment

Many women recalled a point in their drug-use career
when they realized that they had better stop before it became impossible to do so. Some women responded by cut-
ting down, or often by temporarily ceasing drug use. Others
sought professional assistance and entered drug treatment
programs, afraid that they could not do it on their own. All
of the women in this study, however, ultimately continued

using crack cocaine. Those women with a drug treatment history were often motivated by external circumstances, including court-ordered drug treatment in lieu of incarceration, encouragement from health and social services providers, pressure from relatives, and threats from other drug users and sellers. In some cases women were driven by internal pressures such as physiological and psychological problems, pregnancy, "burn out" from drug addiction, or having "hit rock bottom." Other studies have reported similar findings among drug users (Rosenbaum, 1981; Biernacki, 1986; Hubbard et al., 1989; Skoll, 1992). Temporary structural factors also motivated drug treatment admission. These included intensive police presence, extensive and disruptive neighborhood renovations, and seasonal changes.

External Forces

Criminal Justice Involvement and Court-Ordered Drug Treatment

Arrest and incarceration were among the many risks the women in this study faced on a regular basis. These events were most common among the Hookers and the Hustlers. Teranda, who after her arrest lost custody of her three children, saw her apartment lease revoked. In addition, the escalation of her crack cocaine habit created difficulties with her credit card hustle. She said:

> Common sense tells you that you can only push so far. Addicts always think that they can push further than anybody else, and that they won't be caught. The rock does that to you all the time. After you have had some, you want it more so badly that you do stupid things. I went into a store with a stolen credit card after I'd been bingeing for two days. It didn't take a smart detective to bust me. My boyfriend watched from the other side of the store, and he got out of there before the police came in. He was getting on my nerves, and I knew we

were pushing it too far. It almost felt good to be busted because now he could see for himself that he should have stopped me from doing it. They pulled up my record. I lost my three children to the system. The judge said he wasn't gonna let me out this time, and he told me to get my ass in treatment or be ready to spend a few years in jail. At first I told my lawyer that I'd rather go to jail, but then I took the treatment.

Women like Teranda entered drug treatment to avoid incarceration.[3] To receive a suspension of their criminal sentences, they had to complete drug treatment. Although most women voluntarily chose drug treatment over incarceration, at the same time they felt coerced into drug treatment, believing that they did not really have a choice. Others, who were not ordered by the court into drug treatment, were nonetheless often involved with the criminal justice system at the time of their admission. They entered drug treatment as a stalling or diversionary tactic during the pre-sentencing period, while on bail, or after sentencing. Many believed that criminal sanctions would be reduced if they showed their commitment to becoming drug free.

The Hookers were more likely than the Hustlers to experience multiple arrests in a short period of time. Their prostitution was more public than most of the income-generating activities of the Hustlers. Hookers often worked on strolls known to the police, which made them easy targets. Once law enforcement began concentrating on a particular area, women feared being charged not only with prostitution but also with parole violations. They hoped that entering drug treatment would help them avoid incarceration.

Once the women were in treatment, they often tended to be apathetic and reluctant to get involved in program activities. Several women participated only minimally, showing up for required meetings but little else. Others became more interested when they realized that the program might have something to offer them. Then they would begin to reflect on the chaos and stress in their lives and to contemplate the benefits of recovery. Women who developed a trusting relationship with a counselor spoke often of their intention to stop using drugs. Liz, who realized that she was losing her talent as a shoplifter and whose judge offered her a choice between drug treatment and incarceration, liked what her counselor taught.

> When you have to be somewhere, you might as well get the best out of it. They was teaching us all kind of neat stuff, like how to find healthy vegetables and how to cook, being a good mother, like what you have to do for your child, and taking care of yourself, like taking a bath or talking with the counselor.

Foxtrot, one of the Hookers, also became interested in drug treatment through her relationship with her counselor, the first person she had trusted in a long time.

> My counselor knew I did not care one bit. I'd be sitting in her class or in her office and it'd be like she was not there. She didn't give up. We got into this huge argument, and she was talking about me abusing myself. I started crying and told her about all the times that I've been raped. She was the first real person I'd seen in a long time, and I'd do anything for her. I wish she was here.

Foxtrot was not the only woman to point out that drug treatment offered an opportunity to break out of her social isolation, to interact with others. Gail, for example, talked little, but she enjoyed listening to the other women in her program.

> I had like this wall around me, and I told the judge I didn't care what she was going to do with me. She put me in treatment, and my probation officer told me that was a waste of her tax

money. In the program, I'd always be asking questions, but I would never talk about myself. Who cares anyway? I didn't show it, but I was listening to what the other chicks were talking about. They were like me. I got into it, but I guess not enough to make it through the program and stay clean.

Hearing the stories of others made many women realize they were not alone in experiencing confusion, pain, and suffering. Women in mixed-gender programs tended to lack connections with male clients and often felt disrespected and mistreated by the men. Cari, who had been in the same inpatient program four times, explained that same-gender groups could be problematic as well.

Don't get me wrong. Part of it is the program, and part of it is me. I'm not strong enough to take the good parts and run with those. At first we had groups with men and women. One time, I was making this guy cut though his own bull, and he got mad at me. He knew I had used to turn tricks and he yelled at me, "Why would I listen to a whore? Go sell some more of your pussy." The counselor didn't do anything, and most of the guys were laughing. The other women were shocked, and we talked a lot about it. Now we have groups with just women, but it doesn't make it much better. Women are even harsher with each other because being with other ladies makes it more difficult to cover it all up. You learn that you can make it, if you put other folks down. It breaks me down.

Intervention by Service Providers

Once identified to social and health service providers as drug users, the women in project FAST found their lives more carefully scrutinized. Being labeled as drug users led others to view them with suspicion. Some of the women's health care providers believed drug users seldom or never appeared for an appointment, were often late, delayed seeking health care, failed to respond to symptoms, and failed to follow treatment regimens. Some health care providers acknowledged that these negative assumptions led them to approach drug users with limited expectations and interest. They kept their medical obligations to a minimum.

The women, for their part, often entered a clinic or other health care setting anticipating a lack of respect and full of mistrust. Paula, a white Hustler who had ulcers, described a negative encounter with her doctor. When he confronted her with test results of cocaine metabolites in her urine and threatened to report her to the legal authorities unless she sought drug treatment, she felt coerced.

> I was sick like a dog all the time. I know I have ulcers. I'd go to the doctor and he'd write a prescription before I finished talking. He'd tell me what to do and to set up another appointment. I told him that it was difficult for me to do all the things he wanted and asked if I could go to a clinic or something. One of the tests showed cocaine, but he didn't tell me about it at first. He'd be asking me questions, and I'd be lying to him. One day, he showed me the results, and I got very pissed with him. I told him to stay out of my business. He told me I'd better shut up, or he'd have the police investigate me. He scared me, and I went into a treatment clinic. It was worse than prison. Like they take all your self-respect, and you never have time to yourself.

Other women had similar experiences, although it was more common for health care providers to use more subtle methods to motivate the women to seek drug treatment. Nola, who sometimes worked as a prostitute to support her own and her partner's drug habit, recalled intervention by one of her children's teachers.

> My daughter took some rock with her when she was in first grade and showed it to some kids. The teacher found out about it and called me into her class. She's a real bitch. She told me she could've called the police. I started crying, faking it, and

told her I was waiting to go into a program. She got involved, and I had to go.

The women in this study often held mixed views of service providers, seeing them as supportive but also disruptive. Most providers had enough power or control to intimidate and coerce women into entering drug treatment programs. While some women complied with the service providers' demands, others tried to deceive them or, when possible, to replace them with a new provider. Gloria got tired of the nurse at the local clinic where she went to get contraceptives. The nurse sought help from a friend to ensure that Gloria had a place in drug treatment. When it was time to go, Gloria decided not to check in.

> I told you, no more children for me. I need to learn to take care of them. I use rubbers and take that God awful pill. Both are a hassle, but, hey, a woman gotta do what she gotta do. I just can't get pregnant again. I don't go to the community clinic. One of the nurses was gonna save me, and she talked one of her sweet friends into getting me a spot in her program. I did want to go, but something happened. I don't need her telling me I screwed up. It's a pain to have to go downtown to get the pill.

Even though some women entered drug treatment on the initiative of a service provider, few of them actually completed the treatment program.

Intervention by Relatives

Relatives often pressured the women to seek drug treatment. Frequently, the women's relationships with their relatives were strained because of their drug use, their involvement in criminal activities, their chaotic life style, and the stress they caused in their relatives' lives. Several women described their relatives as more supportive than they themselves would have been in the same position. Wendy, a white Hooker, described the chances her mother gave her.

> I am the one who did it to myself, but my mom thinks it's all her fault, like she should have moved out of the neighborhood or watched me all the time. I tell her that me using has nothing to with her, but she won't accept it. I lost all the respect I ever had for myself. It started with stealing some of her money to go get some rock. One time I took this guy with me over to the house to get some of her savings for rock. He walked out with her TV and sold it. I got a hit from the rock he bought with it. I didn't go see my mom for weeks, but she knew I was around. You see, it's hard to hide in a small neighborhood like this. We ran into each other and we made up. I took some more of her money, and she found out about it. She never checked her savings, and I told her I would have paid her back later. She told me to get myself checked into a clinic, or she'd call the police on me.

Other women also mentioned that such confrontations with relatives motivated them at least to explore drug treatment options. Frequently, the women's relatives acted as codependents, a situation of which several women took full advantage. For example, they pleaded for money or clothing, or they turned to relatives when they needed a meal or a place to stay.

The coaxing of relatives had a much more profound emotional impact on the women than did the efforts of service providers. However, many women also knew that their relatives often were more tolerant than their providers. To escape pleas by relatives, several women cut ties with their families. Yet when they found themselves with nowhere to go, they often returned home.

Cheating Dealers and Users

The illegal nature of drug use, its associated lifestyle, and social isolation from non-users all meant that these women's social networks consisted largely of drug users. Typically, social relations were based on shared interests in getting high. Drugs frequently served as the primary glue in the women's social ties, which resulted in tentative and fleeting relationships. Their desire for drugs often caused members of such social networks to cheat on each other by stealing drugs or failing to share them equally.

In the chapter on their relationships with significant others, many women indicated that those partners were typically drug users as well. Several women became tired of the constant fights over money and drugs and of their partners' manipulation of them. Others, however, feared their partner's violence and some sought relief from their partners by entering drug treatment. Martha, introduced to drugs by her boyfriend, had experienced only problematic relationships with other drug users. She viewed drug treatment as an escape.

> My partner knew I had to have some stash somewhere, and he started beating me up to get it from me. He knocked me out and looked all over. I didn't have the stash in the house. The beating scared me, and it started happening more often. I decided to get myself some treatment because I was afraid he'd kill me.

Other women entered drug treatment to escape abuse by a dealer for whom they worked. Angie, a successful dealer, felt that the man for whom she worked was setting her up for trouble.

> I sell ready rock for this guy, and he's always bothering me. He can't stand that I am a better dealer than he is. I pay him his

amount after I sell the rock. He told me I was twenty bucks short, and I know that was not true. He put the word out on me, and I checked into the program so he could cool off.

The women viewed inpatient and detoxification programs as temporary safe havens. Many women spoke of situations in which they had betrayed their dealers or other users because their craving for drugs was stronger than their loyalty to others, including friends. For them, drug treatment provided an escape from people they had deceived, long enough, they hoped, for the betrayed party to forgive and forget.

Internal Factors

Health Issues

Several women had various physical symptoms that worried them. These included trembling hands, heart palpitations, diarrhea, cold sweat, dry skin, urinary problems, angina or heart attacks, seizures, insomnia, paranoia, and having the "bugs" (itching and craving). Typically, they attributed their health complaints to crack cocaine use and tended to ignore symptoms. Tashia, recently released from the hospital after experiencing heart trouble, had this experience.

It had been going on for a while. Any person that has smoked a rock can tell you that they start sweating, get a cold nose, and have cold hands and feet, grind their teeth or bite their tongue, have to shit, and feel their heart bouncing through their body. Crack is hard on your heart. Most of the time I can't sleep, and I started noticing that my heart beat would be slow and get fast and get slow and get fast, even if I wasn't smoking. I thought it was the monkey messing with me. I had an attack or a seizure or something, and they had to take me to the hospital.

A number of women sought drug treatment, hoping the temporary break in crack cocaine use would cure their health problems, but they had no intention of becoming drug free.

Pregnancy

In chapter 4 the reproductive decision-making and the views of motherhood held by the women were discussed. Those women who wanted to be "good" mothers believed they would have to be free of drugs to do so, and they often viewed drug treatment as an effective means to achieve this goal. For a substantial number of women who wanted to be mothers, the discovery of their pregnancies served as a positive turning point. Laura, a white Hooker raised in a dysfunctional family, talked about her wish to be a good mom and to establish a happy family.

> I never much thought about my life until I was pregnant. I knew I wanted the baby if for no other reason than to show the world that I was no different from other women. I tried to quit by myself, but that was tough. I'd be sitting home, thinking about getting high. Like I was obsessed with it. I asked some other ladies, and they told me about the program I went to. By the time I got in I was seven months. I learned a lot about myself in treatment. They sent me home with the baby, and I wasn't ready for that. After three days I was getting high, and my baby has been with my mom ever since.

Laura's experience shows the need for continued treatment after giving birth. Most frequently, the women needed support when returning to their "old" communities, where they experienced "triggers" related to their earlier drug use. Laura continued:

> It was hard for me to come back home and I knew where I could go and get a rock in a second. One of my friends came

by, and she gave me her pipe. I kicked her out of my house
and told her not to mess with me. She thought that she was
being nice. The baby was crying all the time, at least it seemed
that way. It drove me nuts. I was afraid I would hurt the baby
or do the wrong thing. I graduated from the parenting class
but it's different when you have a real baby and you're by
yourself.

Other women echoed Laura's experience. While their
pregnancies motivated several women to seek drug treatment, the treatment seldom prepared them to remain drug
free or for their parenting responsibilities, two challenges
they needed to tackle simultaneously.

Burning Out and Hitting Rock Bottom

Several women in this study reached a point where they
saw no way out and feared for their lives. Most drug users
reach a point of feeling burned out, of having hit the bottom (Biernacki, 1986). Rita, one of the African American
Hookers in this study, feared she would die if she was unable to change her life.

I lost everything I had. It all went into the crack pipe. Like
when you suck it, it sucks your life, but you are too busy to
notice it. I'm not even sure I still am a human being with the
way I am leading my life. I need to get out of this mess, or
I'll die.

Natasha realized that her crack cocaine habit harmed
her, and she wanted to break out of her current way of living as a Hustler and user.

I've been raped by half the neighborhood and had sex with the
other half. I sold everything I had, and I'm going insane. I've
nothing to lose and nothing to gain. If I ever want to respect
myself again, I better get myself out of this mess. I've done
things that the devil wouldn't even think of.

Such realizations compelled several women to seek drug treatment on their own. They usually turned to inpatient drug treatment, followed by continued participation in outpatient programs. Inpatient programs allowed them to create a physical distance between themselves and the drug scene. Some women tried quitting drugs without assistance from a formal drug treatment program by participating in a twelve-step program, or totally on their own with no assistance at all. Patrick Biernacki (1986) described how the heroin users in his study were able to recover "on their own." Dan Waldorf, Craig Reinarman, and Sheigla Murphy explored self-recovery among cocaine users and found that individuals who had "something at stake" often were more successful in controlling their use or becoming drug free.

Most women in this study were skeptical about the potential long-term effects of drug treatment. The more treatment experiences the women had, the more ambivalent they tended to be. The literature supports the view that this ambivalence may result from the negative external factors that motivated the women to seek treatment in the first place (Ball et al., 1974; Hubbard, et al., 1989). Several women in project FAST, especially those who received public assistance, reported that their drug treatment experiences allowed them to gain control over their crack cocaine habit, enabling them to maintain their current way of life.

Barriers to Entering Drug Treatment

Several women confronted waiting lists when they sought drug treatment. They learned that months might pass before treatment slots became available. Women who signed up for treatment and were placed on a waiting list often continued to use drugs during the waiting period. Once an opening became available, some no longer were "ready" to give up their role as drug user. Yvette, one of the African American Hustlers, demanded on-the-spot treatment.

> A person, man or woman, needs treatment when she is ready for it. I have been on about four waiting lists, and every time I relapsed before it was my turn. By the time they were ready for me, I no longer was ready for them. You need it when you need it. It's like a cancer. You have to treat it right away.

Kaishinta continued to use drugs but tried to cut down on her intake, hoping this reduction would allow her to be ready when a place became available.

> This is my second time on a waiting list. The last time, I blew it right away. I couldn't believe they wouldn't take me once I told them I was ready for it. This time I was better prepared. I did not use anything for about a week . . . a few joints, but no rocks. I'm smoking again, but I try to keep my habit down so I can at least make up my mind when they call.

A number of women reported that the wait for publicly-funded drug treatment, which sometimes exceeded six months, was much longer than for privately-funded programs. However, they could not afford the expenses associated with private treatment. Desiré, who at the time of her need for treatment was the partner of one of the largest drug suppliers in town, entered a private drug treatment program. She did not have to wait but, like the other women in this study, she relapsed.

The availability of local inpatient treatment slots for women is small compared to the number of places available for men. This imbalance may result partly from the perception, which was common until recently, that illicit drug use is a male problem. The fewer places for women may also result from an unwillingness and inability by drug treatment programs to provide for women's special needs. Women often require additional social, psychological, and specialized medical services (Inciardi, Lockwood, and Pottieger, 1993). In addition, few drug treatment programs allow women to bring their children, forcing them to choose between themselves and their children. Annika, an African American Hustler and mother of three, contemplated her options.

> I have three children. One child lives with his grandmother, and I get to see him about three times a year. My mother doesn't want me to be around him too much as she sees me as a bad influence. The other two are living with me. If I can get in, I may make it with my two kids and have a nice family with no drugs. They are still young, and I want to get out of this mess before they find out what is going on. The oldest, he is four, was given a demonstration with a pipe the other day. That did it for me. I can get in one program pretty soon, but there's no space for the kids. I'd either have to get my mother to take care of them or give them to a foster family. I don't want to give them to my mother or to a stranger because I may never get them back. There's a program for women and children but it takes at least another five months before I can get in. I don't get it. Everyone is worried about the children, but they'd rather take them away from you than have you work through this mess as a family. I think I'll wait for the women's and children's program.

The infrastructure of drug treatment has a number of inherent structural barriers to female clients, regardless of their motivation to seek treatment. Many women in this study faced additional barriers upon entering inpatient programs.

Experiences with Inpatient Treatment

In general, the women in project FAST agreed that inpatient drug treatment was more disruptive than outpatient treatment, but their expectations of the latter were so low that many believed it was not worth trying. Their general assumption was that if women really wanted to quit using crack cocaine, they should enter an inpatient program. Despite previous negative experiences, many women hoped that a "guided" exit from their role as drug users would be possible, and they acknowledged that previous efforts may have been unsuccessful because of lack of commitment on their part. They also noted that giving up crack cocaine, or drugs in general, was a major step requiring strength, commitment, and multiple efforts.

Once they were in drug treatment, the confrontational approach in the individual as well as in the group sessions disturbed several women. When they challenged treatment staff, they were told that aggressive methods were needed to "break through their shield." Research has shown, however, that such confrontational approaches may be inappropriate for women in drug treatment because they experience more guilt and shame than their male counterparts (Berenson, 1991; Ettore, 1992; Pape, 1993). Drug treatment programs for women should address the women's low sense of self-worth rather than contribute to their negative self-images.

Those women with previous drug treatment experiences emphasized the importance of the orientation of the programs. They preferred approaches that viewed them as more than mere drug users and acknowledged their other social roles as well. Several drug treatment programs are shifting in this direction. One staff member from a local drug treatment center explained:

> We like to respond to the needs of our clients. One of the upper-level staff always seems to be attending some kind of workshop that deals with improving drug treatment. Just to give you a sense, during the last three months one of the staff

members attended training to discuss sexual abuse, transitional treatment, violence and injury control, nutrition, parenting, and the impact of health care reform on drug treatment. We have implemented several of the programs, and the daily structure for our clients has changed drastically. The program activities used to be mainly limited to drugs, but now we provide training and skills in almost all other aspects of life. The way in which we approach all this is that the person first has to go through a four- to six-week substance abuse program, which subsequently is mixed with more non-drug-related components.

According to treatment staff from various other local inpatient programs, the main emphasis of the curriculum remains on substance abuse.

Conversations with counselors often revealed a lack of preparation for their jobs. The majority of the sixteen counselors who were interviewed for this study were former drug users who often lacked formal training in substance abuse counseling or related fields. Although several counselors had completed minimal course work or had participated in workshops, few were certified. Many attended Alcoholics Anonymous or Narcotics Anonymous meetings. Several women felt compelled by their counselors to utilize the twelve-step recovery process even though they themselves had reservations about such self-help programs.

Many women who had inpatient drug treatment experiences complained about their highly structured and restrictive atmosphere. They often failed to understand how such rigid environments could accomplish their goals of becoming drug free. From their perspective, the chasm between program life and real life was too wide. Tina, a Hooker who was ordered by the court to enter drug treatment, was expelled from her inpatient program after twelve days. She said:

I've been in treatment before, and I've been in the joint before. I couldn't tell you which one is worse. In the program I was not allowed to call my boyfriend. My bed and closet were checked about twice a week, and I was never good enough for my counselor. If you'd say something back they'd take your phone calls or something else like your pass away. I'd break their rules all the time, and I knew they would kick me out of there. I'd still like to cut down, so I guess one of these days I'll go back. Maybe I'll try a different program.

Other women were expelled because they smoked tobacco secretly, left the facilities without a pass, used drugs, or had sex with a male client. They perceived drug treatment as an artificial setting, where they always had to be on their best behavior and where they were not allowed to engage in activities they certainly would encounter outside the program.

In addition, several women complained about a double standard, with restrictions imposed on them but not on male clients. To protect female clients from sexual overtures and harassment from men in the treatment center, staff often restricted their freedom. For example, women had to be in their dorms by 10:00 P.M. while men had no curfew. Some of the women found it unfair that they were required to take more classes—parenting classes, for example—than men were. Often they felt the treatment staff had little faith in their potential as mothers. The few women who had been able to take their children with them into drug treatment were dissatisfied with the children's drug education. Sally, whose six-year-old son resided with her in a treatment program, said:

How the fuck can I work on myself and think that I am a good person who needs some help if some bitch is teaching my child that I have a big problem and that I need help? The other day Freddie and I were playing outside, and he wasn't paying at-

tention. I'm helping him to do the same thing for a while.
They told us in parenting class that it is important to teach
your child to stick with something for a while, that way they
learn how to concentrate on a task. I got after him, and he told
me, "Mommy is sick. You are an addict." It blew my mind, and
I started crying. Here they are telling my son that his mother is
a failure. I thought this program was going to bring us closer.

The majority of the women in this study failed to complete their drug treatment. Others graduated but relapsed
after returning to their old environment.

Relapse

The women's accounts demonstrated the difficulties of making the transition from user to non-user, especially if they
were entering treatment for reasons other than perma-
nently getting off drugs. All of the women in this study relapsed and continued to use. The reason most frequently
given by those women who truly *did* want to give up drugs
was the lack of a "safe" aftercare environment. Some
women who were drug free for a limited period of time,
sometimes for up to five months, were frustrated by their
continued stigmatization as drug users. Shirley, who was
drug free for almost twelve months, including three months
in treatment, said:

You never get away from it. No, it's not because I'm afraid
someone will find out, but so many people know about it, like
folks in the neighborhood and the people in the program.
They ask you on your job application, and I will not lie about
it, but I also write down that there is a difference between using and being an ex-user. The only job I could get was as an
outreach worker working with addicts and AIDS. It wasn't
what I had been hoping for, but I figured it was a start. It's a
hard job. You see all the misery in life. My sister got killed, and

my house got broken into. It was too much for me, and I
started smoking again. It's not the smartest thing to do. Maybe
I can hang in there next time.

Shirley's experience is common. "Once a drug user, always a drug user," was a recurring phrase in the women's narratives; researchers have called this perception a "hangover identity" (Ebaugh, 1988).[4] Many women in this study expressed the hope that one day they will be able to remain drug free. They acknowledged that the chance of this happening was primarily in their hands. Other women shifted their expectations to gaining control over their crack cocaine habit.

The Future of Drug Treatment

The women in project FAST were asked to provide suggestions for improving drug treatment programs. The majority preferred inpatient programs combined with methadone maintenance or outpatient aftercare. Many women viewed drug treatment as a major step toward abstinence or controlled use. One of the most frequent suggestions was that inpatient programs should not be mixed-gender and should have a women-focused orientation. The women believed that programs for women only would facilitate more open discussions about such issues as intimate relationships, standing up for oneself, and sexual history, including abuse. They also emphasized the importance of allowing women to bring their children with them and shifting the primary focus of treatment from their own recovery to building families. Individual treatment plans in which women have a voice in determining the order of the issues to be addressed were frequently recommended. Natasha, who earlier in this chapter referred to having hit rock bottom, explained her needs, beyond learning to cope with her drug use.

> Treatment is important because you have to learn how to organize your life again. My main problem was not the crack but the way I was paying for it. I was more ashamed about having sold my body than about smoking rock. In the program, I had to take classes about what drugs do to your body and your mind. I don't care about the chemistry. I needed help dealing with the things I had been doing. I tried to talk with my counselor about it, but she told me I had to finish the drug classes first.

Marta learned that she needed to address her history of being sexually abused before being able to focus on other aspects of her life.

> One of the counselors was like a preacher. He'd always quote something from the Bible. I had been raped, and he made me feel like it was my fault. He'd say that a woman who smokes crack gives a man the wrong impression. As if I had been asking for it. When my new woman counselor and I finally started talking about rape and sexual abuse, I started understanding myself better. I wish I could have learned about that right away.

These experiences suggest that substance abuse should not dominate treatment plans to the exclusion of other issues that are often equally important. Many women with previous drug treatment experiences were more interested in learning vocational and interpersonal skills. Their primary needs centered around survival in a world that offered them little in terms of housing, employment, and personal happiness. As one woman said, "I don't know what substance abuse treatment is supposed to be treating, but I know that it ain't just substance abuse."

Not only did the women address the need for a holistic

approach, one that would acknowledge all of their social roles, they also stressed the importance of aftercare and the involvement of their social support networks, including relatives and friends. Several women mentioned that relatives, friends, or neighbors who knew about their crack cocaine use were sometimes reluctant to intervene. Rita gave an example.

> My sister knew I was getting high, but she'd never say anything. I'd go into her bedroom to take a hit and walk into the kitchen all geeked up. Inside I wanted her to say something because I needed someone to talk with. I couldn't bring it up myself. She couldn't do it either. She'd make remarks about my dirty clothes or my hair but never about the drugs. I stole money from her, and she still wouldn't say a word. She doesn't want to talk to me. I called her from the program, and she wouldn't come to my graduation. When she found out I was smoking again, she told a friend, "She's a piece of shit anyway. What do you expect?" If we just could talk about it.

Others suggested linking drug treatment to other health and social services. Finally, some women recommended the establishment of "low-threshold" drug treatment centers, programs they could enter before being drug free. Some women expressed the wish that such centers, which preferably would be community-based, could be used instead of waiting lists. They viewed these centers as offering transitional programs that allowed individuals who were contemplating drug treatment to prepare for such programs.

Doing It On Your Own

A number of women in project FAST reduced or temporarily ceased their drug intake without assistance from formal drug treatment programs. Because of disappointments with drug treatment, some women believed that only they themselves could quit for good. Overall they agreed that efforts to reduce or quit a drug habit succeed only when persons are ready to do so. Some women preferred to do this "on their own." Patrick Biernacki (1986) has described this approach as recovery without treatment. Other investigators have called it "maturing out" (Winick, 1962; Prins, 1995). None of the women in Project FAST managed to give up her drug habit. Several women, however, especially among the Hustlers, tried to keep their habit under control. Astrid, a Hustler who used to smoke at least $200 worth of crack a week, now spends $50 a week.

> At first I was doing the usual thing. I'd get high and feel half-way decent, I'd come down, and I'd feel like a sick dog. It's like the circle thing . . . I tried to cut down many times, and it didn't work about as many times. I finally did it. I set money aside for the rock and once it's gone, it's gone. I still get drunk when I can't smoke, but I'm working on that too. Once my money is gone, I don't go out as much, and I stay away from the places where you can buy some. Just give me some more time.

While women like Astrid did not intend to quit using crack cocaine or other drugs altogether, they did not want their drug use to dominate their lives. They believed that the key to success was a woman's own strength, something drug treatment in its current format was unlikely to give them.

6 Female Drug Users and the AIDS Epidemic

HIV and AIDS were all too familiar to most of the women in this study. The AIDS epidemic either directly or indirectly affected their lives. Many women knew people infected by the virus, some of whom were symptomatic and very sick. Others had lost relatives, friends, or acquaintances to AIDS. This new infectious disease has posed many challenges to the biomedical community.[1] Despite the investment of years of research and millions of dollars, scientists have identified no cure. Recent statistics from the Centers for Disease Control and Prevention reveal that the greatest increase in HIV/AIDS now occurs among women, especially young women of color (Novello, 1995; Worley and Fleming, 1997). In the United States, most AIDS cases among women result from heterosexual transmission of the virus, with shared needles among drug users the next most common method of transmission. Between 1984 and 1994, the percentage of AIDS cases among women in Georgia increased from 4 to 18 percent. In Fulton County, where most of the women in project FAST lived, the HIV infection rate is 155.2 per 100,000, one of the highest in the country.

A majority of the women in project FAST had been tested for HIV infection; approximately 10 percent had positive test results. Those whose partners injected drugs were often at risk for infection because of the frequency of un-

144

protected sex, the level of infectiousness of the male partner, and the susceptibility to infection among the women (Johnson and Laga, 1988; Padian et al., 1990). Several women had partners, children, and relatives who tested positive as well.

Despite the presence of the AIDS epidemic in their lives, many women were not fully knowledgeable about the disease. Similarly, their perception of their own risk for HIV infection was often inaccurate, and they continued to engage in high-risk behaviors. Public health messages tend to focus primarily on homosexual and injection drug use-related risk behaviors, which can create a false impression that the disease does not heavily affect crack cocaine users. In fact, crack cocaine and its potential link to HIV infection failed to receive attention until the late 1980s (Sterk, 1988; Fullilove et al., 1990; Chiasson et al., 1991). Subsequent prevention campaigns have been derived largely from public stereotypes of crack cocaine users as extremely sexually active with multiple and often anonymous partners. The sex lives of many women in this study, however, especially the Queens of the Scene and the Hustlers, did not fit such images. Many Hookers and Older Struggling Rookies, on the other hand, did engage in high-risk sex acts. Mandy, a thirty-one-year-old Hooker who had previously snorted cocaine and smoked marijuana, worked as a street prostitute for more than five years prior to using crack cocaine.

> I've been turning tricks for a long time, and I have the routine down. If a guy can't come, tough shit, that is his problem. I learned really quickly that crack turns on the brain cells, but not a dick or a pussy. There's this cultural thing that you have sex when you smoke crack. I can't explain why that is. I always go to the same house to smoke, and we don't have any of that crazy sex stuff going on. My old man and I sometimes

> smoke together. His thing is shooting up though. He doesn't
> want to use a rubber because he can't come that way. I use
> rubbers with my tricks, but when I need money very badly I
> may not push for one.

Data gleaned from observations and interviews in this
study reveal that much of the women's sexual activity was
unrelated to the purported aphrodisiac effects of the cocaine. Instead of sexual desire, power differences between
men and women accounted for most of the sexual activity,
and women were the vulnerable partners. Informal interviews with male crack cocaine users who frequented crack
houses where sexual activity occurred confirmed this finding. Jam T, a crack cocaine user in his mid-twenties, offered
this insight.

> Crack doesn't turn me on. I never get a hard-on when I take a
> hit. I love the feeling right after you take a hit. It blows your
> mind. You feel like a piece of shit when the monkey is coming
> down your back. It makes a man feel angry and frustrated. I
> can't stand myself when I am acting like a wimp because I
> can't get high no more. I grab myself one of the girls and start
> messing with her. That way I can feel like a man again.

Other male and female crack cocaine users validated Jam
T's experience. Findings from other research confirm that
female drug users often lack sufficient control in their relationships with men to negotiate safe sex (Amaro, 1988;
Kane, 1991; Deren et al., 1993). Several women initiated
sex in a crack house with other women in order to protect
themselves from demeaning sex with demanding men.

Knowledge, Risk Perceptions, and Actual Behaviors

More than half of the women in project FAST learned of
HIV/AIDS in the late 1980s, while others remained unaware
of the epidemic and the possible ways in which it might

affect them until the mid-1990s. Despite extensive educational campaigns, many women in this study held misguided perceptions about the details of HIV transmission, risk behaviors, and risk-reduction strategies. The women's most common source of information about AIDS was someone who was infected with HIV. Foxtrot, an African American Hooker, spoke in the previous chapter about a positive relationship with her drug treatment counselor. She also described how she first learned about HIV/AIDS.

> We knew there was some kind of bad disease going around, but I didn't pay much attention to it. They is always telling us something is bad. I'd heard people talk about the virus and AIDS and that stuff, but I couldn't have told you what it was at the time. Two of my brothers died of the virus. They was shooting up. I've another brother in California who messes around with guys. We don't talk, but he could have it too. My old man is sick with it, and he also got it from the needle. He didn't find out until he had a hard time breathing, and they told him in the hospital. Now I know about the virus. Several other folks have it, and I am in this program where we bring food to women who can't take care of themselves no more.

Other women in this study realized that HIV infection was a serious health threat once they were directly confronted with its impact. Several women learned of HIV/AIDS from local outreach workers and public health advertisements on local radio and television. Very few ever read brochures or other written educational materials on HIV/AIDS, a finding consistent with other studies (Mays, 1989).

Many women had inadequate knowledge of HIV transmission, believing that casual contact with infected persons might cause them to get the virus. Misty, one of the Queens of the Scene who viewed herself as knowledgeable, said:

> Bullshit, they don't know enough about it. Like they say kissing is safe, but next thing you know, someone got it from kiss-

ing. Or like the thing where some folks got it from the dentist or something. I ain't believing anybody. We should be nice to a person who has it and help that person? Heck, not me. They don't know if you really can't get it from touching a person or using the same toilet. I ain't using no fork that a sick person has put in their mouth.

Other women in this study shared Misty's view. Many feared that the medical establishment lacked sufficient understanding of the disease to provide correct guidelines for risk reduction. A number of women especially questioned public health suggestions regarding safe behaviors. For example, they expressed doubts that HIV truly could not be transmitted by casual contact. They also had doubts regarding French kissing and insect bites. Other researchers have reported similar reservations among their study participants (Flaskerud and Rush, 1989; Harrison et al., 1991). Many of the women in this study also believed that they could look at a person and determine his or her health status, including HIV infection. Several women used a physical assessment, a "quick look," to assess a person's HIV status.

A number of women believed that a cure for AIDS was available, and they referred to media reports and documentaries on television about available medications.[2] Very few women, however, recalled the name of a specific medication. Some women had heard of HIV clinical trials and believed that these were curative.

In general, the Hookers seemed most knowledgeable about HIV/AIDS. Misty has already explained that to survive as a prostitute, she needed to take care of her body. She had regular medical exams. The Queens of the Scene and the Hustlers often viewed themselves as "above risk." The Older Struggling Rookies were not only novices to crack cocaine use but were also the least likely to use condoms as protection against sexually transmitted diseases, including

HIV. Women with a history of injection drug use, typically Hustlers and Hookers, knew they faced risks through the sharing of syringes and other injection equipment. But women with blisters and burns from smoking a hot crack cocaine pipe who engaged in fellatio seldom realized that this practice might place them at risk for HIV infection.

Despite their varying degrees of knowledge, few women reported using condoms consistently. Their continued risk taking seemed related to their inability to assess their own risk for HIV infection. Almost one-half of the women in this study thought themselves not to be at risk. They perceived their own risk as lower than that of their peers; yet they were seldom able to justify this belief.

In addition, as explained earlier, several women felt that they lacked the power and control to persuade their sex partners to use condoms. However, some women were more concerned about short-term needs in their lives than they were about the risk of contracting AIDS. A number of women who knew people who had died of AIDS believed that because they were alive and felt healthy, they were not at risk. One woman had seen a TV show about long-term survivors, people who had been infected with HIV for over a decade. She claimed to be one of them.

The women's failure to protect themselves consistently did not mean that they never attempted to prevent risky encounters. Many women indicated that they and their peers changed their behaviors in an effort to reduce their chances of becoming infected. They most frequently mentioned behavioral risk reduction in sexual rather than drug-use behaviors. The sexual behavioral modifications included decreasing the number of sex partners, reducing involvement in high-risk sexual behaviors, and more frequent condom use.

Detailed probing during the interviews showed that

many women were describing intended rather than actual changes. In reality, many of them failed to translate their intentions into action, especially when engaging in sex prior to, during, or immediately after crack cocaine use. They explained that their craving for crack cocaine often caused them to be less selective with their sex partners, particularly their casual sexual partners, and more willing to engage in high-risk sex acts. Sandra, an African American mother of three who hustled to buy things for her children as well as to support her crack cocaine habit, explained the impact of her drug use on her sexual behavior.

> Sometimes I have sex because I like having sex. It makes the high better. But I also have sex so that I can take a hit like when I give a guy a blow job. He comes, and I suck his crack pipe. I have been needing a hit so badly that I would suck guys that I should have stayed away from. Only when I need to get high badly do I do it with a guy who's new in the house or who smells. I think about myself as a picky lady, but needing a hit makes me be less picky. With my steady, we may do it all the way and we'll take a hit when he's inside me. It makes us both feel good, and I let him come wherever he wants . . . in the front or in the back. There are a few guys in the house that I fuck around with. We lay down on the mattress, and they know I want them to put on a rubber. If they catch me at the wrong time . . . [laughs], I guess it's at the right time if you ask *them*, I let them get away without a rubber. The rock messes it up.

Several women told stories similar to Sandra's about sex under the influence. Their own crack cocaine use, they said, made the sexual encounters less pleasant, mainly because the drug tensed their muscles. By contrast, marijuana and alcohol use prior to or during sex frequently had a disinhibiting and relaxing effect and enhanced the sexual encounters. While many HIV risk-reduction messages target the link between crack cocaine use and sex, alcohol rather than crack cocaine led many women in this study to be less selective with their sex partners and less likely to use a condom. This is especially true for women who drink alcohol to ease their craving for crack cocaine or to reduce the crash after a high. Valerie, the white Hustler who smoked crack cocaine shortly before delivering her baby, offered the following thoughts on sex under the influence.

> It took me a while to figure it out, but for me, the booze is worse than the rock. I drink when I can't get my hands on some rock, and I drink when I just can't get high no more. The booze doesn't make me feel good about myself. I don't care. When I smoke I'm more careful, more tense. I can't fool myself. You can ask people about this. I come across as a tough cookie as soon as I hit the pipe. When I'm drunk, I get soft.

Alcohol-related sexual activity, according to the women in this study, should not be ignored in HIV transmission. Several of them believed that alcohol-related sex alleviated their risk, mistakenly thinking that alcohol killed the virus.

Issues surrounding condom use also were central in the women's narratives. Although very few women had seen or touched female condoms, they often perceived these devices as demeaning and impractical. Hence, the women's comments were limited to male condoms. The main motivating factors for asking male partners to use condoms were to reduce the risk of HIV infection and, to a much lesser extent, to prevent pregnancies. At the same time, they listed many barriers to condom use, including structural barriers, such as the lack of access to condoms, and relational barriers, such as their inability to discuss condom use openly, the emotional and physical distance created between the sex partners by condoms, and the fear that proposing condom use would trigger a violent reaction from their sex partners.

Many women feared that asking their steady partners to use condoms might lead to abandonment, and that their paying casual partners might terminate the sexual encounters and their subsequent access to crack cocaine. Other studies have also shown that from an emotional point of view, the negotiation of condom use with steady partners was more difficult than proposing condom use to casual partners (Campbell, 1990). Relationship dynamics appeared more central to condom use than the women's or their partners' drug use.

Some researchers have found that women are often forced to obey their male partner's wishes regarding condom use (Worth, 1989; Campbell, 1990), while others have found that women do have some influence on the outcome (Kline et al., 1992; Sobo, 1995). The stories of the women in project FAST revealed similar contradictions. In addition to personal characteristics and choices, some women listed their marginal position in society as a main contributing factor in their inability to stand up for themselves. They saw their lack of control as independent of their crack cocaine use. Especially among the Hookers, women believed their fate was largely determined by poverty. Similar findings have been reported by other investigators (Singer, 1994; Farmer, Connors, and Simmons, 1996). Other women indicated that their emotional dependence prevented them from acquiring power in their relationships. In Foxtrot's view:

> I love him. He is my man. He loves me and I'm his lady. We don't need rubbers because we are together. I'll do whatever he wants me to. He never would want something bad to happen to me. If he is serious about the relationship, a condom should not be necessary because I am his only woman.

A number of women did acknowledge that their drug use was a major barrier to condom use and that they sometimes used their partners as an excuse for their own actions. As one of them stated:

> It's different when we wanna get high. You want the drugs and the sex. It's like a way to really get close. I ain't gonna mess with a guy and tell him I want the sex and not the drugs. Guys don't go for that. I mean I want the drugs too. I'd use a rubber, but like I told you, guys don't want it and I ain't giving up no high for no guy.

In addition, some women feared negative repercussions if they proposed condom use. Mandy commented on proposing condom use to her partner.

> A man can't help himself, and I know that they do things to show off to each other. I told my old man that we only do it with a rubber. He got mad, and I explained to him that I know how much he loves me. I also know that he may have sex with other chicks to show his buddies that he is a man.

A few of the women accused their partners of infidelity when the men proposed condom use. Valerie had the following experience:

> He told me that he got rubbers from this worker from the health department and that it would be good for us to use a rubber when he comes inside me. I told him to fuck off. He ain't fooling me. If he has the guts to mess around, he should have the guts to tell me.

Much of the confusion surrounding condom use relates to the distinction many women made between love and sex. To understand the women's perceptions, as well as actual condom use behaviors, one has to consider the role of condoms in the crack cocaine world, gender relations, cultural issues, and economic factors. According to most women, negotiating condom use was much more complex than merely asking a man to "put it on."

Issues Surrounding HIV Testing

Reasons for Testing

Although HIV testing became widely available in the mid-1980s, opinions regarding its value have remained mixed. If a cure were available, positive test results could motivate individuals to seek medical intervention. But since there is as yet no cure, HIV testing primarily serves surveillance purposes. Most women in project FAST had at least one HIV test, and approximately 10 percent of them identified themselves as HIV positive. Very few of these women sought testing voluntarily. Most commonly, they were tested for HIV upon arrest or admittance to an emergency department, hospital, or drug treatment program. Many women received limited pre-test counseling. Angel, a white Hooker who was tested in prison, remembered:

> They tell you that you are gonna get the test, and you have to sign for them telling you. It's not like you can say that you don't want it. It's like a routine, so you can't sue them. It is not because it's good for you. The nurse asked me if I knew about HIV and AIDS and how people could get it. I nodded, and she went on telling me about sex and condoms. It didn't even take five minutes, and she never asked me if I had any questions.

Other women also felt manipulated into taking the HIV test and often lacked the power to refuse. Few of those tested received their results, many having left the institutional setting by the time results were available. Several women in project FAST were tested up to five times before they found themselves in a situation where they got test results and post-test counseling. For many women, seeking their test results was as involuntary as seeking the HIV test in the first place. They listed several reasons for not want-

ing to be tested, including the lack of a cure, a distrust of the
health care system, and fear of legal repercussions. Reasons
for distrusting the health care system ranged from familiarity with public health experiments that involved poor, minority populations to a general alienation from society,
largely the result of involvement in illegal activities (Corea,
1992; Ward, 1993). Pregnant women and women with
young children primarily feared that positive HIV status
could result in the loss of custody.

The women in project FAST considered ignorance of
their HIV status a relief, or as one woman said, "not having
a bad dream." If they didn't take the test, then they wouldn't
have to face the possibility that they were HIV positive.
Mary, one of the Older Struggling Rookies, knew several
people who had died of AIDS. She explained her preference
for not knowing her HIV status.

> This neighborhood is bad news. It has drugs. It has guns. It has
> AIDS. People around here are sick. I know four people who
> died of the package [AIDS]. My next door neighbor gave me
> her pipe. The guys up the street give me rocks. I do sex, blow
> them [fellatio] . . . I never touched no condoms. We didn't
> grow up with that kind of stuff. I think I have the virus, but I
> don't want to know if it is for sure. As long as I don't know, it's
> one less thing to worry about.

Lisa, whose parents moved to Atlanta from Mexico, had
been tested four times for HIV, but she never sought her
results.

> Why would anybody want to know? It's not going to do any-
> body any good. It fucks with your mind, and you might die
> from worrying. I would want to know if there was something I
> could do about it, but not now. I have my tubes tied, so I don't
> have to worry about getting pregnant. I work with johns [pay-
> ing male sexual partners]. They can take care of themselves.

> They know they are seeing a hooker. If they don't want to
> catch it, they ought to take care of themselves. As long as I'm
> healthy, I could care less.

The stories of other women reflected similar cost-benefit analyses. The main disadvantage of not knowing their HIV status, according to these women, was the constant anxiety about the possibility of being HIV positive. The main advantage of knowing their HIV status was that they no longer had to speculate about the outcome. The women in project FAST often had health complaints, which they typically linked to their drug use even when the symptoms were typical of HIV infection.

Several women believed that knowing they were HIV negative served to motivate them to reduce their chances of becoming infected. To be diagnosed as HIV positive, they said, would make them feel responsible for preventing the transmission of the virus to others. However, many women who used this reasoning did not seek an HIV test or the test results. In addition, existing research shows that HIV testing does not necessarily lead to behavioral changes (Coates et al., 1988; Doll et al., 1990).

A number of the women had partners who wanted them to have an HIV test. Often these men inferred that their own status must be the same as their partners', especially when their partners tested negative.[3] Gloria, a white Hooker who described herself as a good mother when she was not getting high, tested negative for HIV. She recalled her partner's reaction.

> We had many fights about rubbers because I knew he was
> messing with other women. I would nag him all the time, and
> he finally told me to get tested if I was that worried. I found
> out about this place where you can get the test, but it's like
> confidential. I almost went crazy when I was waiting for the

test to come back. One day I told myself I had to go in, and the next day I'd tell myself that I didn't have to go to find out about the test. I didn't go when they told me to come in, but I did go later. The test was good. My old man didn't get it, and all he could say was, "See, I told you, you was just being jealous. Now, you know that we don't have the virus."

The main reasons given for wanting to know their HIV test results varied but, as described later in this chapter, these were often linked to reproductive decisions.

Waiting for Test Results

Among those women who were tested and who wanted to know their HIV status, very few were prepared for the waiting period between having their blood drawn and learning the results, which they described as very difficult emotionally. Donna, a twenty-four-year-old Hooker who had had six partners in the past year, two of whom she knew to be injection drug users, was tested voluntarily in a local anonymous testing facility.

> I told you how hard it was to make myself go get the test. I'd been in for the test three times already, but I didn't go in to find out about it. I'd go to different places. I never was sure I wanted to know if I had the bug in my blood. Why the fuck would I want to know if there's nothing the doctors can do about it? This time I did it. Too many folks are getting sick, and the best business around here is the funeral home business. It made me very nervous, and I'd get high just to forget about the test, or I'd be angry and just do whatever. I had more sex without a rubber in those two weeks, but the test was negative. I mean that is great, but now I have to go back in because I screwed around when I was waiting to find out about the bug.

Predictably, the more a woman expected to be HIV positive, the more tormented she became during the waiting time. For a number of women this anxiety translated into increased HIV risk taking. Women frequently saw this period as their last chance to have an identity as a healthy person. Even if a woman felt healthy, getting a positive result marked the end of her disease-free status, if only in her own eyes.

Other women reduced their HIV risk taking during the waiting period, sometimes even ceasing drug use. Xandra, a thirty-year-old African American Hooker, said:

> I knew I had the virus because of everything I'd did in my life. Several of the guys I used to get high with passed away, and last week one of my sisters passed away. All because of the virus. Part of me knew it was too late, but I have not had sex or touched a pipe since last week. It may be too late, but if the test is good, I'm gonna try to keep myself from getting the virus. The waiting is much more scary than giving them a tube of blood.

During the waiting period, the women commonly failed to tell others in their social networks when or whether they had taken the HIV test. If no one knew they had been tested, they maintained, then they would not have to reveal the results in the event the test was positive.

While the majority of the women in project FAST talked with relatives and friends about HIV/AIDS, these conversations were seldom personal. Typically, they discussed HIV/ AIDS in general terms and emphasized the ways in which the epidemic affected others. They considered it inappropriate to ask friends and acquaintances directly about their HIV status. Sometimes they would ask a sex partner about his status, but this posed challenges similar to those regarding condom use. Only a few of the women who were waiting for their test results told others about this. As one woman explained, "It's too close to home when you are waiting for the death verdict."

Negative Test Results

AIDS and its consequences had become a daily feature of the lives of the women in this study. The epidemic seems to be concentrated in inner-city neighborhoods made up primarily of single female heads of households and their families. While the majority of the women in project FAST were HIV negative, the indirect impact of the AIDS epidemic on their lives is often ignored. Ms. Jackson, a grandmother in her early fifties, began caring for her five grandchildren after her daughter died of AIDS. She commented:

> AIDS is a sign from God to show the devil that he will not be able to survive. My grandchildren had to see their mother die. The father of two of them was shot in front of their eyes. The oldest is thirteen, and the youngest is two, and they have seen about everything there is. They are great kids and I pray to God that nothing will happen to them.

Belinda, a mother of three young children, did not use drugs but lived in one of the study neighborhoods. She talked about AIDS in her community and about how the epidemic indirectly affected her life.

> Life is tough if you have to make it on a welfare check, and when you have to look out for your life. I can't let my kids play outside because of the violence. Folks are dying right, left, and center from the AIDS. You see young people walk on the street, and if you didn't know better, you'd think they were at least sixty years old. I can't get close to a man because of the virus. AIDS is on my mind all the time.

Mary, who tested HIV negative four months before this interview took place, made the following point:

> At first, when the nurse told me I didn't have it, I felt like someone told me I'd won the lottery. I thanked the Lord because he wasn't gonna make me die right then. Now it worries me. I have nightmares about getting the virus. It's much worse now that I had the test. Before, I didn't know if I had it, but

that was almost easier. I'm a crack head, but as far as sex goes, I'll always use a rubber if we do it all the way. With blow jobs, I sometimes use a Kiss-a-mint condom, but not all the time. I want to find myself a nice clean guy and live a long life. You know what? There ain't such guys around here.

For several women like Mary, the initial thrill and relief of being HIV negative often led to frustration in trying to remain that way. Frequently, their efforts strained the women's personal and sexual relationships. In order to remain HIV negative, their sexual partners also had to be negative, and they had consistently to engage in protected sex, itself surrounded by tense negotiations. For reasons of love, economic needs, and violence, the women feared challenging their sex partners. In turn, several steady male partners assumed that they were uninfected as long as their female partner tested negative for HIV. This assumption severely hampered the women's attempts to propose risk-reduction measures.

Among the HIV-negative women involved in steady relationships with HIV-positive men, both partners tended to be more willing to practice safe sex. Several women in these couples, however, engaged in unsafe sex nonetheless. Brenda, an African American Hustler, was involved with her partner for three years when he found he was HIV positive. She explained:

Our life is a mess with the drugs, and now he has AIDS on top of it all. We have gone through a lot of trouble together, and I told him I want to be with him through all of this. Sometimes we just get high to forget about it all, and we have done it without a rubber. I know it is stupid but I don't care. He wanted to use one, but I grabbed it out of his hands.

Once they learned they were HIV negative, the women's relief often gave way to fears about whether or how long they could remain that way. A negative HIV test result motivated several women to seek drug treatment, to reduce their crack cocaine use, or to increase their involvement in protective sexual behaviors. Several of them felt they had been given a second chance in life. At the same time, they expressed dismay about their inability to stop using drugs or to engage in safer sex consistently.

A few women in this study were angry about having continually to consider the dangers of HIV infection. They challenged HIV prevention messages regarding safer sex. Cindy, an African American Hustler who tested HIV negative twice, nine and three months before this interview, stated:

> If I don't have the virus, why do I have to worry about it?
> This thing should be about people who have it and not about
> people who don't have it. I mean, if I don't have the virus, I
> should not have to worry about rubbers and all that shit. It's
> the infected folks that should worry about not giving it to
> other folks. If someone else has the flu, they tell that person
> to stay away and not make other folks sick. With the AIDS,
> it is like the people who don't have it should stay home so
> they can't get it. It is difficult to tell someone you have it,
> but you could kind of kill that person if you don't tell them.
> It's wrong to say that it is everybody's problem because it
> ain't.

Several women referred to potential tensions between those who were HIV negative and those who were infected. They described how the "fight against AIDS" had become a fight of "us against them."

Not all of the women who received a negative test result accepted this outcome as conclusive. Instead, they expressed disbelief and doubt. Verna, the Hustler who earlier in this chapter talked about the role of alcohol in HIV risk taking, had been tested four times in the past year. Despite consistent negative results, women like Verna developed an HIV-positive identity prior to taking the test.

Others failed to understand how they could be uninfected despite long-term, intensive involvement in high-risk behaviors. Sandra believed that the medical establishment might have reasons for deceiving her. She referred to the Tuskegee syphilis experiment:

> Come on. There is no cure for it, and the doctors don't know what the hell to do about it. All those smart brains, but no solution. They need people to experiment on, and black, poor folks are perfect for the experiments. Like the Tuskegee men. They had to die so they could find out about the syphilis. I read up on those things because you can't trust nobody. The doctors think "Ah, a crack user, we'll get that poor sucker in the study. She won't know." They tell people they is negative and watch what happens.

A few of the women in the study took a negative test result as a sign that they were "untouchable." As one woman said, "If I don't have it now, I'll never get it." In contrast to the majority of the women, they lacked motivation to change their risky behaviors in order to stay uninfected.

Despite the good news that they were HIV negative, many women found that AIDS continued to affect their lives directly, through the threat of seroconversion and, indirectly, through the illness and death of individuals in their communities. Walt Odets (1991), in his study of gay men, refers to these indirect effects as the "secret epidemic." While the lives of many women in this study had previously been characterized by poverty, violence, and substance abuse, they were now confronted with the added threat of HIV and its social and health consequences.

Being HIV Positive

While the majority of the women in project FAST reported an HIV-negative status, slightly more than 10 percent identified themselves as infected with HIV. Most of the infected women learned of their serostatus while other disruptions occurred in their lives, including incarcerations or hospitalizations. Remembering the day she was told about her serostatus, Teranda, one of the African American Hookers, said:

> I was pregnant, but I didn't want the baby at the time. I was getting high and stuff, and I didn't have my own place. I didn't know who the father of the baby was, and as far as I could tell, the baby could be white, black, or Chinese. I was hoping I wouldn't be able to carry the baby to the end. I was rushed to the hospital, and when I woke up, they told me I had a little baby girl. She was tiny, and her weight was not right. They wouldn't let me see her at first, and this one nurse kept on telling me it was all my fault, like the baby being sick and stuff. Next thing I know, they tell me I have the AIDS disease. I couldn't get over it. Too many things were going on. I wasn't even thinking about what AIDS is and all, I just knew I was in deep shit.

Avril, a white Hooker who had learned three years earlier that she was HIV positive, recalled her moment of discovery.

> I got busted because I was doing it all—selling dope, booting, robbing people, tricking. I knew I would get caught, but I couldn't stop myself, I had to chase the pipe. First they put me in the detention center downtown. I have been in the county jail longer than I have lived any other place in my life. They had us take the test, and we had to go take classes about health and caring for yourself and stuff. The day I heard that I was gonna have to spend another four years, I also was told about me having the virus. It felt like the death penalty.

Very few women learned about their HIV status voluntarily. Of those who did, all but one suspected that she was infected. No matter how they learned of their HIV serostatus, the women rode an emotional roller-coaster, experiencing disbelief, panic, anger, and sadness. Because most women were either informed of their status in an institutional setting or sought testing without informing others, they typically lacked social support during this difficult time. Those women who were identified as HIV positive while in jail or drug treatment received social support through groups available in the programs. Glenda, an African American Hooker, learned of her positive status while in drug treatment.

> I didn't know what to do. I kinda knew I had it, but I was thinking maybe I got away from the virus. It's always a shock. I had been in HIV classes, so I knew what my counselor was talking about when she told me the result of the test. I'm tough and don't like people to see the way I feel. No way I would cry around her. The tears were pushing, and I couldn't find a place to be by myself. I signed up for the group, and I learned just from being there. I don't know if I could've made it without my group. I miss them, and sometimes I think about relapsing just so I can go back.

Although support groups existed in the communities in which the women in this study lived, very few of them attended such groups. They feared being identified as an HIV-infected individual, and groups often met in inconvenient locations and at odd times.

Many women in this study denied their positive HIV status as long as they remained without symptoms. Because HIV manifests no symptoms in its early stages, and because it may take years for symptoms to appear, being HIV positive had no immediate or visible impact on the women's daily lives. As Glenda said, "On the inside I was falling apart, but on the outside I looked like I was the most healthy person." Denial, a typical reaction, was facilitated by the long incubation period of HIV, as well as by the complexities of the disease.

Some women associated HIV infection and AIDS with cancer or pneumonia, while others linked the disease to depression and other psychiatric disorders. By connecting HIV/AIDS with certain symptoms, the women were able to deny their own infection and disease. Barbara, one of the white Hookers who had begun experiencing serious health problems, reflected on her symptoms and denial.

> Rubbers, bleach, no sex, no drugs, toilet seats are safe, kissing is fine. I can tell you anything about what to do, and what not to do, but I couldn't help myself. No one ever told me exactly about AIDS. It's like so many diseases. I knew this guy who died of pneumonia, and he had AIDS. I never had any trouble with my breathing. When I started having trouble with my liver, I thought it was from the drinking. It started getting worse, but I told myself my liver was not an AIDS thing. When they told me in the hospital, I still wouldn't believe it. Because the AIDS can be different for many people, you can deny having the AIDS and tell yourself it's just some disease.

As long as the women suffered only minor health problems, they were able to deny their positive status to both themselves and the outside world. Once their health problems become more serious and less episodic, however, denial became more difficult. Some women, when no longer able to deny their infection, sought to participate in clinical trials. They substituted denial of the disease with hope for a timely cure.

Many of the women adjusted to their HIV-positive status privately, without support from relatives, friends, or service providers. Women with social support were more inclined to disclose their test results to those they trusted. Those women who remained in touch with their relatives usually told their mothers or a sister. Two women who had lost contact with their families sought their support upon learning their HIV status. Their relatives, however, distanced themselves, a fact that these women rationalized with comments such as, "I used to steal from my mom . . . I wasted all her savings," and "I got my little sister involved with drugs, and all my children are in foster care." About one-half of the women involved in steady relationships informed their partners, many of whom were supportive. Three women, however, were physically abused by their partners when they revealed their seropositive status. Fear of abuse was the most common reason for not informing their sex partners. Tashia, a white Hustler, explained, "He would beat me to death because he would be so afraid that he gave it to me but he'd tell me that I gave it to him."

Rita, an African American Hooker, explained her reason for non-disclosure to her sex partners.

> A guy who gives you a rock or lets you hit his pipe . . . and do the oral thing does not want to hear about no rubbers. They want to be in charge, and men are used to showing other guys that they are in charge. They know as much about HIV as I do, and I ain't begging them to use a rubber. I feel guilty about it, and since I have the HIV, I only give blow jobs. I don't know what will happen if they find out. There are other girls out there who have it, and when they were found out, no one wanted to even talk with them.

Many women feared the reactions of others to the news of their HIV infection. Avril, the Hooker who thought of HIV infection as a death penalty, said, "I could use a shoulder to cry on, but I don't know what will happen. I don't want to lose any friends over this." Teranda, who found out she was HIV positive when she delivered her youngest girl, feared she could lose her apartment.

> I see how people who have it are dissed [disrespected]. I ain't gonna let that happen to me. Folks don't respect you. I know this one lady who got kicked out by her landlord, she and her three babies.

Many infected women feared the loss of relationships with lovers and friends, the loss of respect, and material losses, including housing. Non-disclosure allowed them to deny their HIV infection to themselves and to others, and to maintain their self-image as healthy individuals. Through that control, they hoped to prevent being stigmatized as a person infected with HIV.

While none of the infected women in project FAST had AIDS, several experienced episodic illness related to HIV infection. Others were asymptomatic, long-term survivors who sometimes had known of their HIV infection for as long as twelve years. As more individuals fall into the category of long-term survivors, HIV infection becomes a chronic disease, and infected individuals are unclear about its exact progress and timing. As long as there is no cure for HIV, however, those infected have no option of recovery. On the contrary, they must be prepared at all times for a health crisis, which may or may not interrupt their lives for an extended period of time. Tashia again:

> I have my own way of doing this. I never think about it as the AIDS package but just one disease at a time. Last year I had a hysterectomy, and I looked at it as just like that; now, they are working on my kidneys, and my eyes are getting bad. I can't let myself think that it is AIDS because there is no medication for it. I have to look at it as one disease at a time. One disease at a time, with a cure for each disease.

Other women responded by living their lives "one day at a time," which allowed them to focus on the present and be less fearful of the future. Living one day at a time is not an uncommon way of life for drug users, as Glenda's outlook demonstrates.

> I never plan my day. I don't need no book to schedule my appointments. I get up every day, and I see what happens. I go to sleep, and I don't think about the next day.
>
> Sometimes I'd be bingeing, and I don't even know if it's day or night. I don't always know where I'd be sleeping or what my next meal will be. If you are poor, you can't do but take one day at a time.

The combination of being a crack cocaine user and being infected with HIV makes for an unsettled present and future. Most of the HIV-infected women in this study were Hookers and Hustlers. None of the Queens of the Scene were known to be positive, although only four of them had been tested. Several Older Struggling Rookies did not return for their test results, while most never were tested.

In terms of their reproductive role, many women found that their HIV-positive status added to an already complex drug-use process. For one thing, they faced the possibility of transmitting the virus to their fetus. While several infected women in this study had HIV-negative children, others had one or more infected children. The future of their children was one of the main concerns of the HIV-infected mothers. Julie, an HIV-positive Hustler with two uninfected children, aged four and six years old, talked about her concerns.

> Two years ago, I found out that I am a carrier of the virus. One of the guys I dated for a while died because of AIDS. We used to shoot up together. I was tested at the health department. All along, I knew I had it. I knew it. I just knew it. I wasn't sick,

but I knew. No matter what, I was hoping that the test would come out good. I was almost nuts by the time I had my appointment. The counselor looked all worried, and he told me I was positive. At first I thought that was good, but then reality sank in. I started crying. On my way home, I bought a twenty-dollar bag [of heroin]. I bought groceries, and I cooked the kids a meal. I didn't want anybody to know because you become like a nobody. They might kick the kids out of school because of me having it. I'm doing okay. The doctor tells me I have to keep my stress down. You tell me how the heck I'm supposed to do that. For a while I went to a support thing. I went in another neighborhood because I'm hiding it. I'm trying to keep it quiet. I can't sleep because one day my children will wake up, and their mom will be gone, gone as in dead. That's my biggest fear. I'm thinking of putting them up for adoption, but I have to find out if I can do that and that they can stay with me as long as I can care for them.

Those women in project FAST whose children were also infected faced the additional stress of knowing that they had transmitted a fatal disease to their offspring. The ages of the HIV-infected children ranged from six months to three years. Typically, the mothers hoped to stay healthy longer than their children so that they could care for them. They feared that if they could not care for the children, no one else would. Jessica, an African American Hooker who became infected with HIV five years ago, described her feelings about her one-year-old son.

Babies get sick all the time, right? Jerry constantly has a cold. If he doesn't have a cold, he has an ear infection, or he has diarrhea. All kids have this, but with him it is different because you don't know if and how he'll get over it. He's pitiful. Every time I look at him, I feel pain, lots of pain, terrible pain. Pain like you can't describe. I'm the one who is responsible for his slow death. He has no life as it is. I'm afraid to let someone else look after him because he needs all kinds of medication, and he needs to get lots of attention. I've cut down on my drugs, but sometimes I can't stand it and I get high. I make a pipe and I blow like forty dollars worth. My T-cell count is still good, and I pray to God that we may die together. I love him, and I never cared for anybody as much before. He helps me. He makes me feel less lonely, and he gives meaning to my life.

Women like Jessica saw no escape from their disease. They often referred to their own life and that of their children as a "slow death."

Very few women who delivered a child knew in advance that they were infected. Cilia, who was in the third trimester of her pregnancy, reflected on her situation.

This is the most scary time in my life, and I wonder, you know, I ask myself, am I doing the right thing? There's no way of telling what is best. No one understands me. I'm an addict who is dying of AIDS, and on top of that, I'm having a baby. The baby has no daddy. I'm the only person. I know that I might not give AIDS to the baby. That would be great, but I have lost faith. I told my mom and my oldest sister I was pregnant. We used to be very close. They put a curse on me. They told me I showed again that I couldn't be responsible. I pray to God, and I read the Bible. Please understand me. I want the baby because it's something special. It's life. I'm thirty years old, and I'm fucking gonna die. I need something I can call my own. Somebody to love. A baby won't walk away from me. I haven't done anything other than reefer in the last two months. I want us to have a few years together. I don't think much about the future. I take life day by day. I'm angry with the world. There's no place for me, and that's why I'm making my own. They won't get rid of me. If the baby is healthy, part of me will stay alive.

The suffering described by women like Cilia is excruciating, and the crises they face are insurmountable. Several women were upset by society's concern with long-term social costs. They felt that society was trying to take away their reproductive rights. Melinda, an African American Hooker whose two-year-old daughter is infected with HIV, argued:

> We are happy together. I didn't do drugs when I was pregnant, and now I never smoke more than one or two rocks a day. That's nothing compared with what I used to do. I could use some help, but people are scared because we are sick. I haven't heard from my mom for at least fifteen years. She doesn't even know about us. All my so-called friends don't talk to me anymore. I feel I made the right decision. Me and my girl are very close. Fortunately, she doesn't know yet what is going on. I hope we can live long lives, but I'm also afraid that once she realizes, she might get angry with me, run away, or something bad. I had people tell me I shouldn't have a baby. Who are they? How come that old people are kept alive with a machine, but a woman with AIDS is not supposed to have children? It's all about morals. It's about making us feel bad.

Most of the HIV-infected women led lives of increasing social isolation. Frequently, they became more spiritual or religious, having been socialized earlier in life with a religious perspective. Despite their drug use, many women remained involved with religion. Kate, a thirty-four-year-old African American mother of two, explained this.

> It is like how can you get high all the time, and mess around, and tell me that you are religious? You see, I look at it differently. I am a believer. I am a very spiritual person, and I believe in life after death. That has nothing to do with what I do right or wrong in my life. I have faith in God, faith in the people around me, and faith in myself. Yeah, it is a sin to get high, and I wish I could stop. The problem is I know what is right, but the damned craving for drugs just kinda takes over for a while. With heroin it was a lot easier. You'd take a hit, and you would be fine for a few hours. With the pipe, you don't have time to put it down. Craving makes you forget everything you learned, but only for a while. When I

go to church or to choir practice, I am a believer who uses drugs.

Several women in this study used their religious and spiritual involvement to escape the everyday reality of crack cocaine use and their positive HIV status. Others stressed the importance of "thinking positive," believing that a positive attitude toward life enhanced their chances of survival.

7 Violent Encounters

Violence was a common event in the lives of the women in this study. Many had been abused as children, sometimes physically, sometimes sexually, sometimes both. During their adolescent and adult years, a substantial number of the women in project FAST encountered abuse and violence at home, often from their partners, and in drug-use settings. In addition, the communities in which they resided frequently were characterized by violence. In some cases, the women's past abuse experiences caused them to engage in behaviors that placed them at risk for HIV infection.

While most of the women in this study were the victims of violence and abuse, some of them also experienced indirect trauma in witnessing the abuse of others. Fewer women acknowledged having been perpetrators, commonly describing their own violent actions as a defensive reaction to abuse by others. Seldom did a woman describe herself as an independent or unprovoked perpetrator of violence or abuse. When discussing violent incidents, the women often provided contradictory explanations of their actions. On the one hand, they saw themselves as victims, but on the other they recognized themselves as important, independent actors. The field notes below illustrate how these contradictions influenced me, the researcher. Lathia, a single African American mother of a five-year-old daughter, hustled and smoked crack. Her life had been difficult, filled with abuse. Her father molested her when she was about eight years old, but because she was embarrassed, she never shared this experience with anyone. She also felt that she might have brought the abuse upon herself. After her father was fired from his job for reasons unknown to her, he submerged himself in drunkenness.

> Lathia told me she did not blame her father for having lost his job, for having become a drunk, for having taken his frustrations out on her. Recently she began dating a man and she described him as similar to every other man she has been with: strong, attractive, and abusive. One of her main goals in life was to prevent her daughter from getting hurt the same way she did. However, sometimes she acted in ways that contradicted this intention. For example, last weekend she went to a crack house and did not return for two days. Her daughter was home alone, with an empty refrigerator and some cereal. This surprised me and I asked if she had not been worried about her child. This caused a defensive reaction, including referrals to her poverty, her abuse history, and her many negative experiences. I knew she wanted my understanding and sympathy and not a confrontation. As it became clear we could not talk calmly, I told her I had to leave and would prefer we talk more about her weekend some other time. It was hard to walk away, but I felt I had to be up-front with her.

Lathia ultimately was willing to discuss the influence of her past experiences on her current life and the ways in which she used the past to justify her present actions. Other women, however, were unable to share past tragic secrets, even over time.

In general, much of the violence in the lives of the women in this study was related to issues of gender as well as to their crack cocaine use. Most of the men in these women's lives had limited options in mainstream society and felt challenged by society's expectations of men. The women explained that sex was one of the few ways in which their partners could demonstrate their manhood. Society's patriarchal orientation justified the men's behaviors and their desire for dominance. The women's acceptance of such gender inequalities allowed for "symbolic violence" (Bourdieu, 1990). As a result of this acceptance, the women experienced feelings of guilt and self-criticism. It is common for women in general to view themselves as responsible for their violent encounters (LeJeune and Folette, 1994).

Drug use was another key aspect of the abusive experiences of the women in project FAST. Despite contradictory findings about the direction of the link between drug use and violence, studies have shown that these two behaviors are closely related (DeLaRosa, Lambert, and Gropper, 1990; Maher and Curtis, 1992). Drug-use settings, after all, are often places frequented by agitated individuals who are craving and using drugs, coming down from a high, and contemplating strategies to get more drugs.

This chapter discusses childhood and adult abuse, domestic abuse, abuse in drug settings, and community violence. Many women in this study had dealt with all four types of violence, with each type of abuse manifesting its own consequences. The final section of this chapter focuses on the impact of the women's abuse experiences on HIV risk-taking.

Childhood Abuse

The majority of the women in this study referred to childhood abuse as one of the earliest traumatic events they could recall.[1] Frequently, women who use drugs have a history of childhood abuse (Bourgois and Dunlap, 1993; Boyd, 1993; Boyle and Anglin, 1993). Almost one in five women in project FAST had been abused prior to the age of ten. The perpetrators of physical abuse were often the women's mothers and, to a lesser extent, their fathers. Many women provided excuses for their childhood abusers, especially for their mothers. They sympathized with their mother's desperate lives, their constant struggles and frustrations. None of the women whose mothers abused them believed that their mothers intended to harm them. As one woman said:

> It was no wonder that things got out of control. Her life was one big fight. I didn't always do what she asked me to do. She had to whip me in shape, but she whipped me a little too hard. I know my mama didn't want to hurt me. It was the anger in her coming out.

The women were less forgiving when the father or another male relative was the perpetrator. From fathers, brothers, uncles, cousins, and boyfriends of their mothers, the women in this study were more likely to receive sexual than physical abuse. Overall, the women tended to provide fewer excuses for their sexual abusers than for their physical abusers. They found sexual abuse to be much more detrimental, often causing them to feel insecure, rejected, and unworthy. In addition, the consequences of their sexual abuse appeared more severe if the abuse occurred at a younger age, particularly between the ages of five and eight, and if it lasted for several months or longer.

Many women struggled with the fact that as children they were unable to stop their perpetrators, despite the reality that most were too young and too physically weak to defend themselves against an abusive adult. Nevertheless, they blamed themselves for having failed to prevent or end the abuse. Of the few women who tried to challenge their perpetrators, none succeeded.

Like Lathia, whom we met in the earlier field notes, a number of the women excused their perpetrators, blaming the use of alcohol and other drugs. They reasoned that their abusers had not intended to harm them and sometimes could not even remember their violent actions. Hence, these women argued, they should not be blamed for their actions. Bonnie, who two years previously had begun smoking crack and bartering sex to support her habit, was physically abused several times by her drunken father, starting when she was five. Her father, however, had no memory of these encounters. Bonnie said:

> I don't know exactly what happened. I think my dad got in trouble at work because he was drunk or smoking pot. My mom and he would fight every Friday because he'd spend most of his pay in the bar before coming home. He would beat her up, but she got smart. She'd hide from him. Several times, he'd beat me up very badly. The next day he'd be mad at my mama because he thought she'd beaten me up. I'd feel sorry for him. I mean, I didn't know why he was a drunk. When he was beating up on me, he'd call me my mama's name. I tried telling him it was me, but he couldn't hear or see. My mama would come fix me up as soon as he was asleep. I know she wanted to help me, but really, there was nothing she could do.

Childhood abuse experiences caused many women to run away from home. Bonnie, for example, ran away when she was eleven. Since then, she has not spoken to her father. Once he no longer was a part of her daily life and after he lost direct control over her, she allowed herself to be angry at him. She did stay in touch with her mother, but they kept their meetings secret from him.

Once they reached adolescence, many women moved in with a relative or friend. Others became homeless, often falling prey to pimps and low-level dealers. Leaving home not only meant an end to the abuse; it also allowed several women to push their negative abuse experiences into

their subconscious. Annika, the thirty-two-year-old African American crack user who earned most of her money
from prostitution and theft from her customers, frequently
cried when recalling her childhood abuse.

> It's hard to talk about it. My father first . . . he would be drunk
> and forget that I was his little girl. My mother screamed in her
> room when she heard he was coming after me. But she would
> not come and help. One time he knocked both of us out, me
> and my mama. He threw me down the stairs, kicked my bones
> till they broke. I mean, kick as in kicking. The next day, he'd
> kiss me and cry about my bruises. That's why I started missing
> school. My mother finally got the police or somebody to take
> my dad out of the house. My brother was the only man left in
> the house, and he was telling all of us that we had to respect
> him. At first he left my mother out of it, but once he was like
> twelve, he started getting into her business too. The only man
> he had seen in the house was my father. He would not beat
> my mom. He'd yell and scream at her and say things that made
> her cry. When I was eight, he started raping me. He thought
> he was a big guy, like raping your sister shows you are a real
> man. This went on for a long time. I'd run away and he'd find
> me, and he'd tie me to the bed or something. I hate men. I
> hate men so much I can't tell you. I know this sounds stupid,
> but I'd love to find myself a sweet man. They'd never stay
> sweet though. I guess I piss them off. Turning tricks means
> nothing to me. Not after all the shit I went through. It took
> my feelings away.

Annika's experience was not unusual among the women
in this study. Many Hookers who were abused as children
dissociated themselves from the sex act, especially with
their paying clients. Several Queens of the Scene who were
abused as children saw their current high status as revenge
on the men who abused them and on men in general. Fewer
Hustlers and Older Struggling Rookies reported childhood
abuse experiences.

Violence in the Domestic Setting

As we saw in chapter 3, most of the women in this study were involved in steady relationships with male drug users. A smaller number were involved with male non-users or female users and non-users. When describing their relationships, many women referred to incidents of domestic violence. Their efforts to define domestic violence often led them to elaborate on the love-hate nature of these relationships. Among same-gender couples, domestic violence was often limited to verbal abuse by both partners. Several non-using male partners went beyond verbal abuse once they became frustrated with the women's inability to stop using drugs. Drug-addicted men, once they began living off the earnings of their female partners, often became abusive as a way to compensate for their dependence. Some men, especially the using partners of the Hookers, were upset and jealous about the women's sexual activities. Ed and Donna, introduced in chapter 3, were one such couple. Other women and their partners encountered violence that was more directly related to the psychopharmacological effects of crack cocaine.

The women's partners were often their main source of social support. As described earlier, most women belonged to fragile social networks, often consisting of other drug users, and many of them rotated from one negative situation to the next. Many left abusive relationships, for example, only to become involved with another violent partner. When abused by their partners, the women in general failed to report the violence to law enforcement officials, partly because they feared discovery of their own or their partner's drug use. In addition, they usually did not expect to be taken seriously. One male partner, for instance, was called in by the police after his partner reported him. He was told to "come pick up that bitch . . . she needed a good beating." Those women who did file complaints learned that the men were seldom prosecuted.

Frequently, the women blamed themselves or their crack cocaine use for their violent encounters. They identified themselves as undeserving women who often failed to follow a partner's instructions, who challenged their partners, or who lived too independently. They viewed their behavior as a justification for the men's abuse.

The childhood abuse of the women appeared to be an antecedent not only to their drug use but also to violent encounters as an adult. Other researchers have described similar patterns (Zierler et al., 1991; Alexander, 1993; Bennett and Kemper, 1993). Diana, abused by her stepfather at the age of seven and involved at the time of this study with an abusive partner, justified his behavior by blaming herself.

> My old man is a good guy. He can't help himself. You know,
> like we'd be messing around, and I upset him. I'm fucked up.
> Being beaten up for me is the same as being loved. That sucks.
> Like I get scared when a person is nice to me.

Diana attributed her inability to form healthy social attachments to her experiences of childhood abuse. Such reactions are common among women who were abused as children (Van der Kolk and Fisler, 1994). Other women responded by becoming violent themselves, often using their drug habit as a rationalization for their actions. Gina, a white Hustler, hurt her partner with a broken bottle after she got tired of being pushed around by him.

> I'm telling you. We'd be the best couple ever if the drugs
> wouldn't mess with us. As soon as we start hitting the pipe, it
> starts. I enjoy maybe two or three hits, but next thing, I turn

into a bitch. I start tweaking [looking for imagined crack on the floor]. It drives him nuts. We start arguing, and he can't help himself. He'll beat me up or do something to shut me up. It's not just him getting mad. The other day I got pissed because he kept staring at me, telling me to sit down and enjoy the high. I hit him over the head with a broken bottle. He was bleeding like a dog.

While Diana tried to avoid violence herself, Gina shunned the role of victim and became a perpetrator. However, when I pointed out to Gina that she had been violent, she strongly disagreed. According to her, violence related to drug use was unreal and therefore did not count. Several women held a similar opinion, stressing that crack cocaine, not they themselves, caused the violence.

The women in project FAST who lived with their children reported another form of domestic violence. A number of these women had abused or come close to abusing one or more of their children. The potential for abuse was often related to the women's frustrations about the difficult task of raising a child, of being a responsible mother. A number of women panicked when their infant or toddler would not stop crying. Some became so frustrated that they failed to approach the situation with appropriate caution. Other mothers experienced difficulty managing young and energetic children, handling personal exhaustion, or appropriately disciplining a child who ignored them. Situations like these sometimes resulted in violence, even though the women had no intention to hurt their children. Some investigators have suggested that the women's own childhood abuse may cause them to be more likely to abuse their own children (Herzberger and Tennen, 1985; Strauss, 1978). While this observation appeared true for some of the women in project FAST, others had childhood abuse experiences that made them more cautious and at times even overprotective of their children.

While a number of women aspired to be good mothers, they did not always succeed in their goal. In some cases, their failure resulted in their losing custody of their children. Because the consent form for project FAST indicated that any mention of child abuse had to be reported to the legal authorities, the women may have downplayed the extent to which such abuse occurred. One woman admitted that she took the pain and suffering of her own abuse out on her children. To avoid seriously harming them, she asked her mother to take care of the children.

Those women in this study who had adolescent children reported some instances in which their teenage children abused them. While female adolescent children were more likely to abuse their mothers verbally, some male adolescent children became physically violent with their mothers. When some of these mothers responded in kind, they saw their actions as self-defense.

Violence in Drug-Use Settings

Those women in this study who had previously used other drugs found that the drug scene changed with the emergence of crack cocaine. According to them, the crack cocaine scene was the most violent of all drug scenes. In his research on the link between drug use and violence, Paul Goldstein (1985) developed a tripartite conceptual framework, distinguishing between violence caused by the psychopharmacological effects of drugs (in the case of crack cocaine, often paranoia and aggression), violence in the form of crimes committed by users to support their habit, and systemic violence that is inherent in the drug scene. For example, many crack cocaine sellers and users carry a gun or other weapon, which in itself encourages outbreaks of violence. A majority of the women in this study knew someone who had been killed over drugs, and one-half of them had witnessed a homicide. Several women explained that crack cocaine makes one feel overconfident and tends to exaggerate feelings of assertiveness and aggression. Most agreed that men were more likely than women to lose control and become violent after smoking crack cocaine, and that crack made men more paranoid than it did women.

Many Older Struggling Rookies faced constant humiliation and abuse in crack cocaine use settings. Despite their awareness of the potential for violence, their craving for the next high caused them to place themselves continuously at risk. The Hustlers and Hookers were less likely to use drugs in the settings where they turned tricks. Unless they frequented crack houses, their violent encounters tended to occur mainly in domestic settings. In the case of the Hookers, abuse by customers occurred frequently. The few Hustlers who engaged in violent crimes such as robberies and assaults encountered more violence than those who specialized in less aggressive crimes. The Queens of the Scene were often coerced into having sex with their male employers and the employers' associates. Their workplaces were unsafe because of territorial wars between distribution networks, potential raids by law enforcement officials, and internal fights among the staff.

Several Queens of the Scene explained that no one was allowed to make a mistake, especially not cooks. When someone did make an error, that person faced serious repercussions, whether dismissal, serious injury, or even death. "Deviant" women were often punished with sexual abuse. Once, when a manager discovered cocaine hidden under the clothes of a female cook, he forced her to work naked for several months.

Natasha, an Older Struggling Rookie, described an hour in one of the crack houses she frequented.

> I got there around five with ten dollars in my pocket. I was only going to get myself two rocks. My body is worn down from all the sex and stuff, and I need a break from the place. I wanted to smoke a little by myself at home. That way you can't turn around and see if you can get another hit from someone else. No one owes me anything because I never have a rock to give away. This one guy always is generous to me, and he doesn't really want me to do too much with him. He saw me and told me he needed a hand job real badly. It turned out he was training some other young chick. I didn't know. Fuck, I figured, I get one hit from him and still buy myself two rocks. After my first hit, I got greedy, and I started looking around to give another hand or blow job. This guy grabbed me by the arm, twisted it behind my back, and forced me to do it with him. Some other chick kicked me in the head because she was hoping he'd ask her. She needed a rock, too. Every time, there's people fighting all over.

Although many women, like Natasha, were abused in each other's presence in crack cocaine use settings, they offered each other little support. At times, violence occurred between two or more women. In one crack house, the men would place bets on tussles between women as if they were cocks in a fight. Research has shown, ironically, that persons who have been victims themselves are less empathetic to others facing the same victimization (Deitz et al., 1982). Very few women in project FAST discussed their violent encounters, especially those that were drug-related. They seldom shared these encounters with each other, and those who did usually confided in female friends. Few women presented their abusive experiences as status symbols. They proudly showed their physical scars, but hid their emotional scars carefully.

Very few women were successful in overpowering their abusers. The most unusual incident involved a woman who bit a man's genitals, while simultaneously protecting her tongue in a condom. Her action, she said, was revenge for all the times that this man and others forced her to have sex with them.

Violence in the Community Setting

Drug users do not live in a vacuum, nor do their lives revolve solely around drugs. The women in this study were relatives, neighbors, friends, partners, parents, and colleagues. Many women stressed the importance to their lives of a community context. Many lived in under-served, violent neighborhoods, and a frequent complaint concerned the lack of police protection in their neighborhoods. As one woman said:

> You don't hear no nothing on TV about a guy getting killed. They'll show it if a white person is involved or if it is someone important. You can go to a funeral of one of the young men in my neighborhood, and there won't be no newspaper people. They show it on TV if a child gets killed, like children are more important. I agree, they are helpless. But you know what? The men and women are helpless too. It's a different kind. There's drug gangs outside my apartment. Most of the guys who are in charge are from other parts of town. They appoint a lieutenant here, who has to listen to them. I've called the police on them, but they never come late at night, and during the day it takes a few hours for them to get here. They had this cop walk around the community, like he was our cop. I think he got scared, because he ain't been back.

In addition to dealing with persistent poverty and a crumbling physical infrastructure, many women routinely witnessed violence in their crack-infested communities. William Wilson (1987) has observed that residents who have the means to move to neighborhoods with more resources do so, leaving the "truly disadvantaged" behind. Elijah Anderson (1990) has argued that the social context of poverty in deprived neighborhoods creates an ideal opening and foundation for the crack cocaine culture. Jill, an African American mother of four children who did not use drugs, was raped as an adolescent by two young men from the neighborhood. She said:

> I used to live downtown. The neighborhood has changed a lot. We used to play out on the street and go visit all the neigh-bors. Everybody knew each other and looked after each other. There were no strangers, and no one had a gun out on the street. I remember new folks moving in, and they were trash. Some people couldn't sell their houses, but they wanted to leave so badly they just left the building. My mom couldn't afford to move. She got on my nerves because she always was scared for me and my sister with all the riff-raff around. I had the late afternoon shift [at a fast food restaurant], and it was almost ten at night. My friend had gotten off earlier. I was sup-posed to call my mom, if there was no one to walk home with me. I didn't want her to come out, and I mean, I thought I knew the streets. About two houses from my house, these two guys jumped on me, and I was raped by both of them. I knew one of the guys from school. You see, I had been flirting with him but I wasn't into any sex or anything. He later told his buddies how he screwed me. My mom had me identify him to the police . . . it was bad. We moved, and I had to go to a different school. I never could see sex as something special. It was a bad thing for me.

Jill now lives in her old neighborhood with her own chil-dren. Every time she passes by the place where she was raped, she relives the experience.

In conversations with these women and other members

of their neighborhoods, some people blamed drug users for the disintegration of the community, while others saw widespread drug use as a result of that disintegration.[2] Streets and parks generally were declared unsafe. In one community, the residents referred to a local park, inhabited mainly by drug users, as "Jurassic Park." As one woman put it, "You go there, and you'll find any kind of monster you have ever heard of."

Not all violence at the community level was drug related. In many of the study communities, youths turned to gangs to give meaning to their lives and to gain status. Few of the men in their late twenties or older were gang members. A street reputation often substituted among the younger men for social mobility in mainstream society. The presence of youth gangs like the Duce Gang, the K-wood Kings, the Drug Boys, the Far Bloods, and the Kool Aid Gang frequently was linked to non-drug-related violence.

A small number of women in this study knew of female gangs, and a few of the younger women were gang members themselves. Female gangs differed from the male gangs, however, in that geographical territory, or turf, was not a priority. Instead, female gang members viewed their gangs as a way to meet members of male gangs or, conversely, to challenge traditional male dominance by imitation. Many residents feared the random nature of gang violence more than they feared violence among drug users. Mr. Johnson, a male resident who had lived in the same community for over fifty years, noted:

> Life sure as heck has changed. When I was a youngster, we were into gangs and fighting and stuff. It's something a young man has to go through for him to grow up. We used to fight over the ladies or what color was the color of our block. It was almost romantic, like showing you were a man. People didn't

get killed. We used to have something to look forward to, and me and my friends would talk about getting married, having a job, buying a car. The youngsters don't have any of that. There are no jobs. Women want a guy to buy them stuff and push guys into hustles. I am afraid of the gangs we have around here. They kill each other. They kill if they don't agree with each other or if another gang comes too close. Someone who is staying by themselves gets killed around here because some kid has to show he can kill someone before he can join the gang.

In his community, men like Mr. Johnson were called "old heads." Typically, these males served as role models to the younger generation, teaching them the value of manhood, employment, marriage, and fatherhood. As the local economy changed, however, young people turned to other role models, those active in the underground economy. "Being a good man" took on a different meaning. In another study, Anderson (1990) described a similar decrease in the prestige and credibility of the old heads, implicating the underground economy, particularly that related to crack cocaine, in the change. The role of old head was not limited to men. It also applied to women who served as role models for younger females. In the changing climate, however, many of these women became socially isolated because they were afraid to leave their homes.

In order to survive, some old heads became involved in the underground economy. Drunk Mama—a female old head who used to be called simply Mama—began managing one of the community's liquor houses, places where alcohol is sold in small units or where customers can buy shots for as little as a quarter. While liquor or shot houses had long been familiar, established sites in the study communities, they became even more common and acceptable in the changed climate of the street. Drunk Mama described her partner's liquor house.

> We had liquor houses when I was growing up. It was a thing for the guys, and the only women that would go there were whores. I used to think it was a bad place, and we used to pray for them folks. With the crack houses, the liquor houses don't look that bad. I was afraid to leave my house. I love gardening, but I could get killed being out there pulling some weeds. I started dating this gentleman who runs a liquor house. It's not his. He's like an enforcer [person who intervenes when things get out of control]. Without him I would be in prison or dead. He made me his main lady and I kinda run his place for him. The guys watch my back when I'm doing my yard. It's a great deal all the way around.

Other residents who were involved with liquor houses only peripherally or not at all still recognized such houses as community institutions. In some ways the liquor houses preceded shelters and food kitchens as social support networks. For example, people who had no place to stay were allowed to remain in the liquor house overnight. Most houses served at least one meal a day. In return for lodging or food, one had to clean or cook. With the onset of the crack cocaine epidemic, the role of liquor houses has expanded. Many crack cocaine users will frequent a liquor house to buy cheap shots of alcohol when they do not have enough money for crack or when they are coming down from a crack high.

Violence and the HIV Epidemic

Much of the focus in this chapter has been on the link between the women's experiences and their perceptions of violence. Clear links seem to exist both between the women's

early violent encounters and their later drug use and between their drug use and subsequent violent experiences.
Findings from several studies indicate that exposure to physical and sexual abuse may place women at increased risk for
HIV infection (Paone and Chavkin, 1993). The stories of the
women in project FAST indicate a possible association between the impact of their abuse and HIV risk taking.

Their experiences with abuse led many women in this
study to dissociate themselves from reality, which in turn
allowed them to deny their involvement in HIV-risk behaviors such as unprotected sex or sex with at-risk partners. Crack cocaine use facilitated their denial by desensi-
tizing them to the sex acts in which they engaged. Bonnie,
the Hooker who earlier described her childhood abuse,
explained:

> It may not make sense to you, but that's the way I am. I talked
> with a shrink about it over in the drug treatment center. I can
> live because I put things away, and it is like it never happened
> or it could have happened to someone I know, but not me.
> There's a name for it. I can't think about myself as sucking
> some guy's dick because I want a hit. That's not me. That's a
> crack head.

Other women used similar justifications for having unprotected sex with casual partners, and used their crack cocaine use as an excuse for engaging in risky behavior. In their
steady relationships, several women needed to smoke crack
cocaine before having sex. The Hookers especially needed
crack cocaine to overcome the negative connotations sex
held for them. While the majority of the women who re-
acted by dissociating themselves from reality were aware of
HIV-risk behaviors and potential risk-reduction strategies,
they seldom protected themselves. One woman said that if

she died of HIV, she deserved it, and that her death at least would put an end to her constant victimization.

The sexual abuse experiences of other women in project FAST rendered them unable to negotiate safe sex. Typically, they were less assertive than women who had not been abused. Liz, who had been physically and sexually abused as a child as well as an adult by her steady partner, talked about her experiences.

> I'm nobody. It's that bad. I never get any respect [laughs]. I guess I don't give myself any respect either. I've been beaten over the head so many times, I've given up. I used to dream about a nice guy, my own house, children, a dog. You mention it. I know about all this condom business and about watching out who the guy is you are doing it with. No guy is gonna listen to me. Why would I ask him to use a rubber and give him a chance to beat me up? If he wanted to use one, he'd pull one out himself. My role in life is to be exploited so that men can feel good.

Liz was far from the only woman in this study who refused to ask a partner to use protection during sex. While these women realized that they placed themselves at risk for HIV infection, they felt unable to change their behavior. Even when they intended to protect themselves, their plans were often undermined by the effects of or the craving for crack cocaine. In addition to the potential trauma surrounding drug use and violence, they had an added fear: becoming infected with a deadly disease.

8 Past Experiences, Future Aspirations and Policies

> The past is the past. I'm glad it is over with. When I was little, my
> mama had to fight to make it. My oldest brother got shot dead. My
> baby brother has life without parole. My memories? It's all bad. It's like
> a pain. Look at me. I had to hustle to make it. Who cares about poor
> black folk anyway? The past is important if people had good stuff hap-
> pening to them, stuff they can be proud of. That ain't me. I never had
> any chance. (Kate, African American Hustler)

Women like Kate found thinking about the past point-
less. Other women became depressed when thinking back.
These women's perspectives on their past, present, and future form the core of the first part of this chapter and are
followed by discussions of the impact of the constantly
changing drug market on their habits and a look at policy
issues and topics for future research.

In general, many of the women in project FAST had
mixed feelings about past accomplishments. A number of
them described dwelling on the past as a typical middle-
class activity, especially common among feminists. Samantha, a Hooker in her mid-thirties, substantiated this view.

> I've been going to the women's center. It's a new place in
> town, like nice, caring, rich ladies who want to get close to
> poor bitches like me. I think it's a joke. But you know, it's one
> of them feminist things. They have groups where you go in
> and you tell your story. The other women listen and you can

cry with them. I did some of that when I was in the treatment program. I'd make my story sound so sad, you can't fucking believe it. I got the counselors crying. The women in my group got mad at the world, and they were bullshitting about sexism, racism, and all that other shit. I lost my cool and tried to explain that I was okay, that I was looking forward to my future, that the past had made me strong. The feminists just wanted to talk about the past, about what all had happened to them, and how they could get back at men. I'm telling you, we all were women, but we sure did not look at the world the same way. We had a psychologist come in, and she'd try all her book stuff with us. It don't work that way.

Although Samantha's experience involved women from different racial backgrounds, most of the women interviewed found such attitudes typical of white women. They also tended to view the practice of psychotherapy as a white, middle-class, feminist approach to coping with the past.

Women who had been physically or sexually abused, either during their childhood or at a later age, were an exception. Many of them, especially among the Hookers, were interested in seeking support to cope with these experiences. Most, however, lacked the means to pay for professional help and wished for informal, cheaper support systems. An informal local prostitution organization provided a support group for women who had been abused. Typically each session was attended by at least ten women, one-third of whom were African American.

Another common feature of the women's views of their past was the tendency to blame external circumstances for their negative experiences. This frequently resulted in limited and contradictory explanations for their life circumstances. For example, several women explained that relationships with significant others had failed because their partners were unable to understand their circumstances or wanted to take advantage of them. Others felt challenged in their role as mothers because of their drug use, even though they saw themselves as adequate parents. Still others complained about drug treatment programs that failed to serve their needs or had unrealistic requirements for enrollment. In time, however, they would to go beyond these initial explanations. Teranda's story is a good example. In chapter 2, she described having high expectations of a male partner. She expected him to be honest and respectful, to provide financial as well as emotional support, and to focus on the family. She had been unable to find someone who met these criteria and was ready to accept her single status as permanent. At one point, after we had firmly established our relationship, I asked her if she had considered lowering her standards. She replied:

> Why is it always the woman who has to give in? Why would I try to fit his ticket, right? Well, I don't want to. I like the way I am. I'm tired of guys using me, bringing shit into my house. I want a guy who is going to make my life easier, not more difficult.

Because she never referred to the impact of her crack cocaine use on the available pool of partners, I mentioned this as a potential area for change. She responded:

> You're right. Maybe I will have to cut down on drugs. If I meet the right guy, I for sure will cut down. I might even quit. You know what, I never thought much about me having to give up drugs first. I mean, I know that is important, but it is frustrating with no good guys around. Drugs make it easier. I hear you. I want to have my cake and eat it too.

Teranda was not the only woman who over time acknowledged the need for change on her part. Often these women were so focused on the impact other people had on their lives that they underestimated their own potential to enhance their quality of life. Kate, quoted at the beginning of this chapter, is another example. At first she singled out racism as the cause of her unhappy life. Several months later, however, when she and I had another conversation about her past, she added that guilt about her own actions made her reluctant to reflect honestly on her life. She had begun injecting heroin in her late twenties and later shifted to crack cocaine. At some point during our conversation, I asked her if she believed drug use played a role in molding her circumstances.

> Drugs is part of the same pain. If a person is poor, that person is treated like a nobody. I always feel put down and drugs gave me a way to feel better about myself. I know not everyone around here does drugs. I don't need you telling me that. Okay, so I'm the one who decided I was gonna use dope. You think that makes me feel good about myself? You think I am proud of that? I'm messing up my life. It's hard to see how I screwed up . . . but it's not only my fault.

Whereas Kate initially presented herself as a victim of circumstances, she later also acknowledged her own role in shaping her life. Ultimately, she concluded that she shared the responsibility for her past and present.

Most of the women in project FAST used past experiences to justify current circumstances. A substantial number reconstructed their past to explain the present. Some women, for instance, revised their past while in drug treatment. Cari, who described her drug treatment experiences in chapter 5, elaborated on how she had recast her story.

> I used to love group sessions. Sitting around in a circle, listening to what other folk went through. It always made me feel like my life wasn't as bad. The one thing I hate about myself is turning tricks. I try to hide it from people. It's the lowest thing a woman can do to herself. Some women just talked about turning tricks in the group. They'd explain that it was because

they was raped when they was young. I didn't have too many
very bad things happen to me, like being abused or something.
My dad ran away when I was a baby, so I figured that's bad.
My mama used to hit me sometimes. My stepdad and I did not
get along. By the time it was my turn to talk, I did not change
my past but I made it sound like it explained why I am doing
what I am doing.

Women like Cari manipulated the past and changed its
meaning to explain their present circumstances.[1] Similarly,
most other women in the study realized that the justifications for their current situations only captured part of the
reality. After several informal and sometimes formal interviews, many women indicated that while their excuses
were real, they themselves also had to take some responsibility for the circumstances of their lives. Like Kate, they
were willing to acknowledge that not all women who grew
up in similar circumstances became drug users.

Those women who perceived their lives as gratifying or
as relatively successful prior to their involvement with
drugs, including most Older Struggling Rookies, often dwelt
on those earlier drug-free times. All of the Older Struggling
Rookies agreed that regardless of the struggles they endured
before using drugs, their lives as crack cocaine users were
even more chaotic and destructive. They often emphasized
past accomplishments from the time before they used crack
cocaine, as in this statement by Margie.

Like I said, I've been poor my whole life. Few people would've
made it with the things I had to go through. I took care of my
children. I raised my grandchildren. It don't take money to
teach them about respect, to teach them to be a good person.
I'm proud of them and myself.

By focusing on their lives before drug addiction, the
Older Struggling Rookies and several of the other women

could temporarily ignore their current circumstances. Bringing the past into the present made them feel more positive about themselves and their lives. During the interviews, it frequently took multiple probes before the women were willing to be open about their present situations. Sometimes they presented long-ago events as though they had occurred recently. Mary, for example, did not use crack cocaine or any other drugs until she was in her late thirties. She was very proud of her job cleaning offices in a luxurious building and said, "Like I told you, it's the job I like. You have your own floor, your own equipment and everything. I like it that you do whatever you want as long as you get the job done." But Mary had held this job more than ten years before. Living in the past made her current chaotic life more bearable, a coping strategy also used by many of the other women.

In general, almost all of the women in this study approached life one day at a time. Wendy, a white Hooker whose mother blamed herself for her daughter's drug use, exemplified this attitude.

> The only way I can make it is to take it one day at a time. Thinking back is kind of depressing for me. Looking at the future is scary. For me, it works best when I'm in between the past and the future. I mean, today, just today.

Like Wendy, many of these women preferred to live in the present, to focus on a limited period of time instead of feeling trapped in the past or overwhelmed by the future. The present was distressing for all of the women in this study, with the possible exception of the Queens of the Scene. These women perceived the present as a perfect time. However, taking such a short-term perspective also created problems for them, most notably for those with children in their roles as mothers. It also caused the significant relationships of many women to fail, especially among women involved with non-using partners, who typically held more future-oriented perspectives. Living one day at a time also served as a barrier to seeking drug treatment. As one woman said, "Just keep asking me. I'm telling you, I'll go to the program tomorrow, tomorrow, tomorrow."

Future Aspirations

In addition to past experiences and current circumstances, the women in this study made references to the future. Many hoped for a future with fewer daily struggles, often without drugs. Even women who failed to take action expected tomorrow's life to be brighter. These expectations were highest among those women who had been raised in families with a quality of life well above their current level. They knew what life could be like. In addition, women who had completed high school or had had positive job experiences tended to be more optimistic about the future. Their past accomplishments reinforced their awareness of options. Thelma was one of the women who expected to have a positive future once she gave up drugs.

> No one can take my high school diploma away from me. They can take everything else, but that's my ticket to the future. I know I can enjoy life without using drugs. I'm still a good hair dresser when I'm sober and take the time. I'm gonna quit using. I just have to do it. I gotta say in my mind that I want to change. I want to do it. I've put it in my heart. That's gonna take me a while cause I don't want no treatment. I'll find myself a good sponsor [as a member of Narcotics Anonymous]. It will take me a while, but I want to have my own store. I know I can do it.

Women who were Hustlers, like Thelma, had the most hope. Despite the fact that the imagined future might be a long way away, they believed that they could reach their goals. At times, they ignored present struggles by projecting themselves into the future.

With the exception of several Queens of the Scene who were proud of having reached the top of the ladder in the drug business, most women assumed they would have to give up drugs in order to have viable options. When asked which aspects of their lives would affect their future options, the women cited having employment opportunities, physical and mental health, and the chance to establish healthy families.

Employment

Many women expected to find regular employment once they were drug free and aspired to such jobs as cashier, hairdresser, cosmologist, switchboard operator, secretary, and nurse. These types of jobs are largely held by women, which indicates some level of conformity among the study participants to gender-role expectations. Other women, whose aspirations far outstripped their training or capability, wanted to be teachers, college professors, or lawyers. Several women received their GED and some college credit while serving time in prison. Positive experiences with drug counselors and other treatment staff gave some women aspirations to careers as drug counselors or therapists.

Women who grew up in families in which the mother or another adult caregiver worked were often familiar with the pressures of combining domestic responsibilities with employment outside the home. They were socialized to value education and employment. Women raised in households in which such behaviors and norms were not valued or taught often lacked the cultural capital to survive in a world that values education and employment.

Many women were angry about the exploitive nature of their mother's jobs, recalling their moms as coming home from work exhausted. Those women with little formal education held the lowest expectations and understood that they might have limited options and end up with jobs similar to their mothers'. Some of the older women had no expectations at all regarding employment possibilities.

Despite their aspirations to seek semi-skilled and professional careers, few women considered the additional education and training these jobs require. For example, a number of women aspired to become nurses, a profession that would allow them to take care of other people. Seldom, however, did they address the years of education that this career would require. Other women received compliments about their hair or make-up and often assumed that they could find employment in the beauty field. Even the few women who acknowledged needing additional training were unrealistic about the feasibility of being admitted to training programs. Cindy, who aspired to become a nurse, said:

> I'm gonna be a nurse. My mom was a cleaning lady in the hospital and when I was little she'd sometimes take me along. I love those uniforms. I know I'll need more than my high school diploma. I never was a good student, but I like helping people. That's important when you want to be a nurse. I know you think that a crack head has no patience, but I have a lot. I don't mind cleaning up dirty sheets and washing people. It'll make me feel useful. I'll have to figure out what school is good for me, but I know I'll do it. Once they find out I really want to

be a nurse, they'll take me. You can come take a picture of me in my uniform.

Although the majority of the women realized that they would have to give up drugs to fulfil their goals, they often ignored other potential hurdles. Cindy said, "Heck, a person who beats ready rock [crack cocaine] can do anything in life." In reality, however, most of them are likely to encounter difficulties in furthering their education or training or in finding employment. Being unprepared for such potential disappointments and having unrealistic expectations will be discouraging, and may even lead to relapse among those who are successful in getting off drugs.

Mental and Physical Health

A number of women in this study believed that the potential to achieve a bright future depended on their mental and physical health. Many realized they were not guaranteed good health, when years of drug had taken their toll. Several women looked forward to feeling proud of themselves if they could kick their drug habit, but they ignored the possibility of long-term psychological consequences resulting from their lives as drug users. Despite a diagnosis of post-traumatic stress syndrome, some of these women believed their symptoms would disappear once they had been drug free for at least one year. About nine months before this study was conducted, after having been clean for almost four years, Candy relapsed. Nevertheless, she is convinced that one day she will overcome her depression and develop stronger self-esteem.

> I've been clean for four years. That's a long time. I had no idea how difficult it would be. I mean, crack was on my mind all

the time. I had constant craving and my counselor told me that
I had the post-Vietnam disease because of all the abuse. I was
building my self-esteem, working the twelve steps, and doing
self-discovery. During the day things were fine, but I'd wake
up every night dreaming about them raping me or something.
I started smoking again, but I know I can do it. I learned how
it feels to go through this. It's not that I'm messed up. I'm depressed right now, but I tell myself drugs are better than suicide. Once I get off drugs, I will feel great.

In terms of their physical health, many women assumed
that their problems would disappear once they were drug
free for an extended period of time. Others believed that
stopping drug use would result in healthier and more attractive looks, which in turn might enhance their opportunities in life.

Establishing a Family

Being able to establish their own families was a frequent as-
piration of the women in project FAST. A majority of the
women dreamed of a fairy-tale ending in which they would
meet a prince on a white horse who would rescue them
from their harsh circumstances. Their dreams included living with their family in a nice house or apartment, having
their own car, buying goods with credit cards, and filing tax
forms. Their aspirations were similar to those of most Americans and reflected middle-class values. Some women presented a picture in which they drove their children to private schools, regularly held children's parties and cocktail
parties for adults, and took a vacation abroad every year.
Shirley, whose previous efforts to give up her crack cocaine
had failed, shared her fantasies about the future.

I'm not gonna be greedy now. I don't need to win the lottery
and be rich. I don't want to be wealthy because you can see on

TV and in the newspaper that most wealthy people are un-happy or have trouble. What I want is to be comfortable. I like a nice clean house, with a garage, a garden, and a large kitchen, the refrigerator always packed with goodies. I'll have two more children, one boy and one girl. They'll have nice clothes, and they'll never learn about poor people's lives. I won't complain to them about where I am coming from. Every year, we'll take a vacation abroad. I've never been in a mu-seum, but that's what we'll do.

Women like Shirley were convinced that once they found the appropriate partner, they would make up for lost time. Several women considered a happy family future with children but no husband. Mandy, a Hooker in her early thirties, wanted to become a mother but preferred to stay single.

There's no way a man can take care of a lady and her kids like they used to do. I'd rather take faith in my own hands. I mean, I like a man to take me out or buy me a present or something, but not to live with. If I have a problem, I talk with one of my sisters [female relatives and other significant women].

A substantial number of women revealed that as they be-came increasingly aware of future opportunities, they be-came more intrigued with the possibility of reaching their goals.

Dead End

Several women, however, lacked any hope for improve-ment and felt desperate. Many of these hopeless women struggled to support their drug habit, often as Hookers and Older Struggling Rookies. Few were involved in steady re-lationships. Most had lost custody of at least one child, without any chance of regaining custody. Some of them were infected with HIV and viewed the progression of their disease as an end to their misery. In the words of Kitty, a woman in her forties who learned of her HIV-positive status almost five years before:

> I can't wait to die. Just get it over with. Why did God put me in this world? I can remember every happy day in my life, because I did not have many. I don't know my dad. My mom ran away, and she'd show up once in a while at my grandma's house. She overdosed. Grandma used to beat me because I looked like my mama. She'd hit me instead of the other kids. I was raped when I was eight. I ran away, and I was taken right behind the dumpster. I couldn't talk about it. My first child died when I was fifteen. She was born with a drug habit. The rest of my life is about being cheated, beaten up, used. I'm a piece of trash. Nobody can change that. You're a sweetheart, but it'd be better if you'd leave me alone. I've been in programs. That's when I really felt like shit. I have the total package [AIDS], and I can't wait to die. Not in no hospital. I wanna die on the street. That's where I have been most of my life.

Other women felt similarly, perceiving themselves to have little or no control over their lives and feeling trapped. Women like Kitty were anchored in the present. They made no attempt to quit using drugs and often failed to see giving up drugs as a way to improve their future. Instead they presented their drug use as a temporary coping strategy. Several women believed that they lived on a dead-end road, with no escape.

Changing Drug Scenes and Aspirations

Crack cocaine was the drug of choice for all of the women in project FAST. The emergence of this drug on the local street market caused one of the biggest shifts ever in the drug scene. For Queens of the Scene, it created opportunities in the drug business. For others, it became an affordable drug, while at the same time it often destroyed their lives. Several Hookers and Hustlers shifted from using other drugs or using different forms of cocaine to smoking crack cocaine. Few of those women who changed drugs chose to do this themselves. More commonly, their drug habit changed because of market dynamics. Desiré, who supported her injection cocaine and heroin habit through prostitution, never intended to begin smoking crack cocaine, but she nevertheless became a crack cocaine user.

> I'd go to Cool T. He used to be my main dope man. He'd always have the best stuff in town. He gave me some rocks to try, like a sample. I'd heard that stuff made people nuts, so I told him I didn't want none. He kept pushing it, so I took a few rocks to shut him up. You see, I'm an addict so I had to try some of the rocks. I didn't feel nothing. I smoked it the wrong way. Cool T. showed me how to do it. Soon I was spending more money on rocks than on my habit. His business made more money from rocks. That's why he pushed it on me, and I'm not the only person.

Desiré said that her life had become totally chaotic and out of control since she became a crack cocaine addict. She said she was on the waiting list for a local methadone program, having decided to seek treatment because she feared becoming infected with HIV if she continued to inject drugs. Once she began smoking crack cocaine on a regular basis, however, she forgot her previous health concerns as well as her intention to change her life. Other women revealed experiences similar to Desiré's. The drug habit of the Older Struggling Rookies was most clearly affected by the drug market. Few of them would have turned to drugs without the aggressive marketing of crack cocaine dealers.

When the women in this study discussed a desire to give up drugs, they often meant that they wanted to quit using their primary drug of choice. As this study was nearing completion, however, new drugs were appearing on the drug market, especially methamphetamine and heroin. Methamphetamine is also known as "redneck cocaine," a reflection of the drug's primary suppliers, who are individuals from rural areas. While methamphetamine is not new to rural drug markets, its availability in urban markets has been limited until recently. Interviews with crack dealers and users and information on local epidemiological indicators of crack cocaine reveal that the market for crack may be saturated. Hence, some dealers have begun exploring new niches in the drug market, methamphetamine among them. Several women in project FAST had begun combining their crack cocaine use with methamphetamine. Nola, an active crack cocaine user, said:

> Of course I'd heard about it, but I didn't know they was selling it. I'm used to pills, like Black Beauties and stuff. Now they are selling the stuff all crunched up, like in small plastic bags, like a powder and you can shoot it. I myself toot [snort] it. This stuff is great. The high is fantastic and you know what, you stay high for a long time. It's like I can enjoy getting high again. I really didn't enjoy rock no more.

Several other methamphetamine users pointed out that a methamphetamine habit might be cheaper and less destructive than a crack cocaine habit. A recurring theme in their stories was that although they continued to use crack cocaine, they no longer enjoyed its effects. Getting high had become common, and it primarily served to overcome the constant craving for more crack cocaine.

Angie, one of the Queens of the Scene, reported that her boss was conducting an experiment in one of his market areas. She described his technique of mixing cocaine with methamphetamine. So far, she said, he was pleased with the promising results. Many users who were unaware that they were buying crack cocaine mixed with methamphetamine provided positive feedback. They particularly enjoyed the longer-lasting high. The decreasing prominence of crack cocaine on the local drug market may create a niche for methamphetamine. Women in project FAST who intended to quit smoking crack cocaine may end up using methamphetamine rather than giving up drugs altogether.

Heroin also has the potential to displace crack cocaine use, at least partially. Crack cocaine users often take drugs with "calming" effects to ease the crash after a crack high. Typically, alcohol and marijuana serve this purpose. More recently, however, an increasing number of women in this study had begun experimenting with heroin as a way of easing the crash from a crack cocaine high. These women's crack cocaine dealers suggested that they try heroin and often provided them with free samples. One dealer acknowledged that shifting his customers' habit to include heroin increased his profits.

The women who tried heroin tended to like the effects. Some sprinkled heroin powder on their crack cocaine rocks and smoked this combination. Others snorted heroin before or after smoking crack cocaine. Still others, although very few, injected heroin. Women in this last group all tended to be new injectors who did not have past drug injection experiences. Sometimes women transformed the crack cocaine into an injectable solution that they injected with the heroin. At this time, no one combination of crack cocaine and heroin use seems to dominate, but heroin is clearly becoming more popular. Its quality continues to improve, while the price has fallen.

As with the impact of methamphetamine availability

and the positive evaluation of its effects, heroin might alter the women's intentions to become drug free. Instead of giving up drugs totally, they may shift from crack cocaine use to drug habits that they perceive as less destructive. These changes in the local drug market have already altered the aspirations of some women. Several of them argued that one of their main reasons for wanting to quit using crack cocaine was its negative impact on their lives. These newly emerging drugs appear to give some women a reason to delay or abandon their plans to become drug free.

Policy Issues

From the point of view of most of the women in this study, society's solutions to their drug use do more harm than good. They believed that forcing women into drug treatment is unlikely to succeed unless the users themselves are ready to give up drugs. While arresting and prosecuting drug users removes them from the streets and keeps them from committing crimes, this approach fails to provide long-term, constructive solutions to drug addiction and its consequences. Treating pregnant crack cocaine users as criminals and forcing them to give up their children is likely to hurt the women as well as their offspring. Welfare reform aims to prevent drug users from using public assistance to support their drug habit. In reality, however, it was welfare dependence that motivated several women in this study to curtail their drug intake. Blaming female crack cocaine users for their sexual promiscuity and the spread of HIV into the general population does not take into account the heterogeneity of these women, nor does it adequately address the complexities surrounding HIV risk reduction. For example, HIV educational materials often urge sexual partners to get to know each other and learn about each other's sexual history and attitudes toward condom use. But what "getting to know a partner" means in the context of the lives of the women in this study is unclear. Even the Queens of the Scene, the most powerful among the women in this study, were in no position to question their male sex partners about past sexual activities.

During the interview process, many of the women in this study became visibly sad as they realized that few solutions to their problems exist. They believed that poverty, sexism, and racism had hurt and continued to hurt them. At the same time, aspects of their stories also revealed the role that they themselves played. In chapter 3, for example, both Valerie and Liz described their desire to nurture their children, to care for them, and to be there when needed. In reality, however, they were often unavailable or preoccupied with their crack cocaine habit. My many hours of babysitting, combined with those provided by some community consultants, could not make up for that lost time.

Discussions with Valerie, Liz, and many other women revealed that they felt caught in a web, unable to break loose. They did speculate about things that could help them to better their lives, things that society could do for them and things that they could do for themselves. They emphasized the need for community-based programs that addressed all aspects of their lives. They proposed a harm-reduction approach, which included low-threshold programs that do not penalize drug users who have not quit totally or who relapse, that provide psychological services to help them cope with their past experiences as well as practical services such as basic education, life-skills training, job preparation, and employment opportunities. They yearned for larger societal changes as well, especially for an end to poverty and an increase in welfare benefits for the poor.

Gender-specific drug treatment programs like those suggested by the women in this study might have higher success rates than traditional modules. But being drug free would not solve all of the problems these women face. Many realized that their options would remain limited and that even if they were able to stop using drugs, they would still have to cope with many other challenges. Even if they returned "clean," their communities remain "dirty." Because crack cocaine dominates the local drug market, a user does not have to seek out copping areas. Crack's pervasiveness makes it difficult for a person to avoid it. None of the Older Struggling Rookies knew how to acquire drugs until crack cocaine became available in their neighborhoods. Nevertheless, all communities had residents who chose not to use drugs. Some of the women who became drug free reported conflicts with these residents, who continued to view them as drug-using pariahs, especially if they had been known to trade sex for crack in the past.

The lifestyle of most of the women in project FAST, even the Queens of the Scene, was chaotic. The Queens of the Scene and many Hustlers held central roles in the crack cocaine business. Without them as cookers, dealers, steerers, and holders, the business would be unable to function. As users, all of these women supported the crack cocaine economy, but this economy also included domestic and international smugglers and producers. Many women felt that drug enforcement policies targeted them unfairly rather than seriously challenging the more powerful players in the game. Arresting Hustlers and Hookers might improve crime statistics and demonstrate local awareness of "the drug problem."

But getting a few drug addicts temporarily off the street does not address the larger problem. There are always more addicts ready and waiting to buy crack, and arresting a few Older Struggling Rookies will not have an impact on the drug business.

There is also the consideration that even if all of the women in this study could quit their drug habit, their lives would remain full of despair. Policy makers who accuse users of an unwillingness or inability to give up drugs frequently ignore their other needs. The "war on drugs" unfortunately fails to eliminate poverty and other social ills.

What Good Would Legalization Do?

The consequences of legalizing drugs must be considered. While decriminalization is often defined as a reduction in legal sanctions, legalization assumes the elimination of legal sanctions altogether. Decriminalization and legalization both have disadvantages.[2] Much of the discussion about the legalization of drugs, including their decriminalization, has focused on its impact on drug-related crime. Some policy makers argue that if drugs are legalized, their price will fall dramatically, simply because of shifts in the market dynamics. Consumers would be more protected, and they would need less money to support their habit, which in turn might yield a reduction in criminal activity. It is unlikely, however, that the price of crack cocaine would drop significantly, considering its current cheap price. Furthermore, the Older Struggling Rookies and those Hookers who depend financially on exchanging sex for crack would not change their behavior, nor impact crime statistics, even if crack cocaine were cheaper. Hookers who exchange sex for money are unlikely to reduce their prostitution, because most limit their drug intake in order to work. A similar stability in criminal involvement might exist among the Hustlers, who also curtail their use in order to perform their hustles. The Queens of the Scene would lose their jobs if dealers were to eliminate their positions as a cost-saving measure. But society at large would barely note any change in the prevalence of crack cocaine-related crimes.

A concern frequently raised in legalization debates is that many non-users might become attracted to drugs once they became legal. But one of the main reasons why the crack cocaine epidemic is leveling off is the drug's negative reputation. People know that crack is a "bad" drug, and that label would probably heavily outweigh any appeal that legal status would give to crack cocaine. Of course some people would be tempted to try the drug if it were legalized, but there is no reason to suspect that this group would be large.

Advocates of legalization assume that crack cocaine users have a right to choose whether they want to use the drug and that they can determine for themselves whether they are willing to pay the potential costs. While public opinion is divided about the desirability and extent of government intervention, none of the women in this study opposed such intervention. They did, however, demand that such intervention be constructive. Their main frustrations and complaints were that government intervention punished rather than helped them, that financial resources were used to build more prisons rather than to improve the physical infrastructure of their neighborhoods, and that money was invested in foster care rather than day care.

Finally, it is argued, legalization might reduce drug users' involvement in behaviors that harm their health. Obviously, continued crack cocaine use has negative health consequences for those who use it. Their involvement in un-protected sex poses a major HIV threat. Some women refer to crack as the "demon." Often the negative side effects of crack cocaine result from chemical additives used to make the rocks appear larger. Some dealers add chalk to make the rocks look whiter, an indicator of purity, according to some users. Other dealers add milk powder, laundry detergent, and a wide range of chemicals. Legalization might facilitate quality control. Many women in this study emphasized the importance of a uniform quality, having become very ill from an unexpectedly high-quality rock or a rock cut with dangerous chemicals.

Many women in this study failed to seek health care be-cause they distrusted medical professionals, whom they perceived to be disrespectful of them as human beings in need of care. They feared being identified as drug users or having to deal with unpleasant or disheartening encoun-ters. If crack cocaine were legal, these women might be more inclined to seek health care, provided that legalization removed the stigma attached to crack users. A better un-derstanding of drug users by health care providers and an increased trust in the medical profession among the women would enhance their involvement in HIV clinical trials. At the time of this study, very few women were enrolled in tri-als. Those who were enrolled in such research experienced difficulty with complicated treatment regimens and some-times used crack cocaine to cope with the negative side ef-fects of the medications. Other women tried to enroll in a trial but were excluded because their heath care provider refused to enroll drug users. But clinical trials are often the only way for poor, HIV-infected individuals to gain access to valuable therapies.

Legalization would also make drugs available in traditional outlets such as pharmacies, community clinics, and drug treatment centers. Many women in project FAST were socially isolated. If crack cocaine were legalized, however, they would automatically be linked to central health institutions that could serve as low-threshold programs and triage the women into other services.

Overall, it seems that the legalization of crack cocaine could be expected to have many advantages and few disadvantages. But legalization alone is not the solution to the wide range of problems encountered by the women in this study. It would not move them out of poverty, eliminate racism, or abolish sexism.

Future Research

The women in project FAST were a unique group. They all were active users of crack cocaine, having been recruited for the study in their own communities rather than in prisons, drug treatment centers or clinics, or other institutional settings. Although the targeted, snowball, and theoretical sampling allowed for the inclusion of a wide range of women, they are unlikely to be representative of all women who use crack cocaine. The goal of this study was to develop a better understanding of female crack cocaine use from the women's perspective. Future research to investigate a larger group of women with a longitudinal design is needed. In addition, researchers should be sensitive to the constantly changing nature of drug-use patterns. Several Hustlers and Hookers would have qualified as injection drug users in the past. Some women appeared to be shifting to combine their crack cocaine use with heroin or methamphetamine.

Many cross-sectional and longitudinal studies on drug use focus on the individual, sometimes in combination with that person's drug-use network. An important theme in the lives of the women in project FAST was the intergenerational nature of drug use. This topic is worthy of more in-depth investigation. Studies also need to focus on the community context of drug use. Such research might provide explanations for why some people from the same community use drugs while others do not.

The women's accounts provided many suggestions for future prevention and intervention programs. For example, early intervention might have led some of them to discontinue using drugs. The women's suggestions for gender-specific drug treatment and other health and social services require further examination. Additional investigations should build on the enormous amount of information on the women's sexual and reproductive decision-making to develop future HIV interventions. A major strength of the study's ethnographic research design was its emphasis not only on the women's perspectives but also their suggestions for gender-appropriate and culturally specific research and services.

In general, the stories of these women suggest that their drug use can only be understood when placed in a larger societal context. A number of them realized that while they had no control over their racial background and gender, they did have opportunities, though against the odds, to change their socio-economic status. This realization led several of the women to conclude that they themselves as well as society must change if their goals are to be achieved. These women who live life in the fast lane know that they must play a role in reducing the turmoil of their lives.

Notes

Introduction

1. The term "crack whore" refers to a woman who provides sexual services, primarily vaginal and oral sex, to male partners who pay for these services with crack cocaine. "Crack freaks" typically are women who engage in sex with other women while being watched by male users who reward them with crack for their performance. "Chicken heads" are women who provide oral sex in return for crack cocaine.

2. To protect the privacy of the study participants, their names have been replaced with pseudonyms. All quotes were taken directly from field notes and interview transcripts. Sometimes the study participants used street and drug vernacular, which frequently is presented in an unaltered format. No information was deleted from the quotes that would alter the tone or intent of a comment. The language has been preserved intact as much as possible, although redundancies, incomplete thoughts, dangling phrases, and digressions have been omitted. Some of the quoted statements, especially those made during informal interviews, are presented as if derived from one conversation, even though they might have transpired over a series of interactions.

3. Many steps were taken to ensure the safety of all members of the project staff, including myself and the community consultants. Most of the time we entered the field in teams of two or arranged for the companionship of a local key informant. Nevertheless, I had several close calls such as the time when a drug dealer was caught ripping off one of his regular customers, who returned with some of his friends to take seek revenge. Other incidents involved fights between women and their boyfriends. Finally, crack houses tend to be unpredictable settings. Sometimes arguments occurred between users who were sharing a supply, with dealers who were unwilling to give crack cocaine on credit, or among sex partners who were unable to agree on the sex-for-crack exchange. Typically, crack cocaine makes its users paranoid, and I quickly learned to avoid situations that could escalate or to leave prior to the escalation. I could not always predict when a potentially dangerous conflict would arise, but I was never physically hurt.

4. The procedures involving human subjects' protection were approved by the Internal Review Board of Georgia State University. The informed consent form clearly described the study. Each woman who was interviewed received a copy of this form, which included my name and phone number. In addition, women were offered referrals to local social and health services and a clinical psychologist volunteered to provide counseling.

Chapter One

1. Reflecting society's norms, many individuals distinguish between "good" and "bad" drugs or between "soft" and "hard" drugs. Marijuana and cocaine taken intranasally are frequently viewed as "good" drugs. The drugs and routes of administration more prevalent among lower class users—such as heroin, cocaine injection, and the smoking of crack cocaine—are frequently associated with social problems such as crime, violence, and the destruction of families and communities. Thus these drug habits are referred to as "bad" and "hard" (Musto, 1973; Reinarman, 1983). These distinctions are socially constructed, as is the "stepping stone" theory, which assumes that once individuals begin using drugs, they are likely to shift from soft to hard drugs (Kaplan, Bieleman, and TenHouten, 1992).

2. For a more detailed overview of occasional and controlled use, see Blackwell (1983), Powell (1973), and Zinberg (1984). Waldorf, Reinarman, and Murphy (1991) describe the experiences of controlled cocaine users. No studies are available on the controlled use of crack cocaine.

Chapter Two

1. For more information on role-taking, role identity, and the prominence of roles, see Turner (1962), Blumer (1969), Hewitt (1984); Stryker (1992), Heiss (1981). These concepts are central to the theoretical framework of symbolic interaction.

2. Despite the success of the Queens of the Scene, they frequently were accorded less status than their male counterparts in the drug business. While women who participate in the legal labor force have the means available to challenge sexual harassment and abuse, such protection is lacking for those women involved in the underground economy. Many women in project FAST reported protecting themselves from sexual harassment and abuse by pretending to be very busy with work activities, never being in the room by themselves, and deflecting deroga-

tory remarks made by any of the men present. Scott (1985) refers to such strategies as "weapons of the weak." However, many of the Queens of the Scene were unable to escape sexual pressures, manipulation, harassment, and abuse.

3. Patrick Biernacki (1979) describes how most drug users will specialize in a criminal activity. He refers to this activity as the "main hustle."

4. Terry Williams, in his book *Crackhouse: Notes from the End of the Line*, provides a detailed description of sexual patterns in one crack house. He discusses how women who are losing control over their crack habit also lose the leverage to make demands of their sex partners. In *Crack Pipe as a Pimp: An Ethnographic Investigation of Sex-for-Crack Exchanges* (1993), researchers from seven metropolitan areas in the United States corroborate this shift in control.

Chapter Three

1. Studies of African American single mothers also show that they tend to have negative views of men. Many women expressed a preference for being single if the alternative was investing more in a relationship than they personally got out of it (Staples, 1973; Wilson, 1987).

Chapter Four

1. With the emergence of the crack cocaine epidemic in the second half of the 1980s and the relatively high participation of female users, legal discussions about the regulation of women's reproductive rights resurfaced. In the early 1990s, ten U.S. states and the District of Columbia had specific gestational abuse statutes (California, Florida, Illinois, Indiana, Massachusetts, Minnesota, Nevada, Oklahoma, South Dakota, and Utah). Six states mandate that health care providers report a neonate's positive drug toxicology as evidence of child abuse or neglect (California, Michigan, New York, Maryland, Oregon, and Connecticut). The State of Georgia lacks a requirement to report gestational drug use, but it does have an implicit reporting requirement. Several counties have formed task forces for such reporting staffed by representatives from the District Attorney's office, the Department of Family and Children Services, the local police force, and local medical facilities. Under the current policies, many counties seek the prosecution of pregnant drug users. Women have been charged with child abuse, child neglect, child endangerment, assault, and delivery of drugs to a minor. Interestingly, the

evidence used to prosecute is circumstantial and indirect and involves the presence of cocaine metabolites in the newborn. In addition to criminal prosecutions, termination of parental rights is governed.

2. In cultures throughout the world, motherhood is viewed as a source of power and respect. Although women in many cultures, specifically in Western industrialized societies, have become increasingly involved in social roles outside the domestic sphere, their role as mothers has remained central. In dual career families as well as in female-headed households, many women continue to make decisions about employment and related activities based on their responsibilities as mothers. The social identity of women in the lower socio-economic strata is affected more by their mothering roles than is the case among more affluent women. Motherhood more than anything else provides meaning to their lives. For recent work on the role of motherhood see Daphne Spain and Suzanne M. Bianchi, *Balancing Act: Motherhood, Marriage, and Employment Among American Women* (New York: Russell Sage Foundation, 1996); Sharon Hays, *The Cultural Contradictions of Motherhood* (New Haven: Yale University Press, 1996); Elizabeth B. Silvia, ed., *Good Enough Mothering: Feminist Perspectives on Lone Motherhood* (New York: Routledge, 1995); Mary K. Blakely, *American Mom* (Chapel Hill: Algonquin Books, 1994); Shari Thurer, *The Myths of Motherhood: How Culture Reinvents the Good Mother* (Boston: Houghton Mifflin, 1994); Ann Oakley, *Social Support and Motherhood: The Natural History of a Research Project* (Cambridge, Mass.: Blackwell, 1992); and Penelope Dixon, *Mothers and Mothering: An Annotated Feminist Bibliography* (New York: Garland, 1991).

Chapter Five

1. Drug treatment has been the topic of heated discussion for more than a century. At the end of the 19th century and during the early decades in the 20th century, many scientists viewed drug addiction as a curable disease (Musto, 1973). Today, the most common treatment modules for drug rehabilitation are methadone maintenance, outpatient and inpatient programs, and therapeutic communities. The ultimate goal of all drug treatment is abstinence but the drug treatment modules vary in structure and length of program. The nature of drug treatment programs often reflects drug trends in society. During the 1960s and 1970s, for example, heroin dominated the drug market, and methadone maintenance programs and therapeutic communities became popular. As other drugs such as amphetamines, hallucinogens, and cocaine became more prevalent in the 1970s and subsequent decades, the number of non-

methadone inpatient and outpatient programs increased. Often, these programs offered auxiliary services such as assistance in finding housing and employment. Some programs also made crisis intervention available.

2. None of the project FAST women mentioned any of the drugs that have proven effective in detoxification from crack cocaine. These include desipramine, amantadine, and buprenorphine (Tennant and Sagherian, 1987).

3. While drug abstinence is the main goal of treatment, the reduction of drug-related crimes is often a secondary goal (Jaffe, 1987; Musto, 1973). The Treatment Alternatives to Street Crime (TASC) programs, established in Chicago, Des Moines, Miami, Phoenix, and Portland with the aim of diverting nonviolent criminals into drug treatment, found that those clients ordered by the court into treatment were at least as successful in completing treatment as other clients (Collins and Allison, 1983).

4. Goffman (1963), for example, also addressed the consequences of social labels and how a stigma never really disappears. Theorists of labeling further confirm the lingering stigma attached to ex-deviants (Lemert, 1951; Schur, 1971).

Chapter Six

1. HIV (human immunodeficiency virus) is a retrovirus that disables the immune system, causing infected persons to be prone to a wide range of opportunistic infections. Under normal circumstances, a person's immune system fights infectious microbes by releasing immunocytes. However, a person infected with HIV is unable to do so. HIV is difficult to treat because the virus mutates quickly. Over time, numerous strings of HIV have been identified between individuals and within persons. Furthermore, HIV poses challenges to the biomedical community because it has an incubation period estimated to be between two and fifteen years. Finally, not all persons infected with HIV develop AIDS. AIDS is a syndrome including many diseases such as pneumocystis carninii, Karposi's sarcoma, herpes simplex, and infections of the central nervous system. In the early 1980s in the United States, HIV infections primarily were identified among men who had engaged in sex with other men. Originally, the disease was called Gay-Related Infectious Disease (GRID). As the virus was found among others, including recipients of blood transfusions, injection drug users, and certain immigrant groups, the name was changed to Acquired Immunodeficiency Syndrome (AIDS). Despite an increase in HIV incidence and prevalence and actual AIDS cases among

women, many still view AIDS as a homosexual disease. A certain amount of this type of ignorance may be expected in the general population; but the research community has also shown little interest in issues unique to women infected with HIV. In biomedical circles, discussion regarding differences between male and female pathophysiology have been initiated only recently. For a more detailed discussion of issues unique to women see Howard L. Minkhoff, Jack A. DeHovitz, and Ann Duerr, *HIV Infection in Women* (New York: Raven Press, 1995).

2. A review of Atlanta area newspapers and TV programs aired during the data collection phase for project FAST revealed that HIV/AIDS was featured numerous times. The availability of AZT, a drug known to reduce the "viral load" (percentage of virus in the blood), was frequently the subject of these news reports. Also discussed were protease inhibitors such as ddI, ddC, and 3TC. As more drugs became available, medical experts began suggesting the use of drug "cocktails"—the combination of several drugs—to slow the progression of the disease. One woman joked about the availability of "AIDS cocktails." The term cocktail is part of the drug users' vocabulary and also refers to the combination of several drugs.

3. This is yet another demonstration of the gender inequality among drug users. The women in project FAST frequently lacked the power and control to speak up for themselves. Despite the progress of the women's movement, many of its gains are limited to white, middle-class women. In order to understand the decisions made by the women in this study, it is important to consider the cultural, economic, and social reasons for their actions.

Chapter Seven

1. David Finkelhor and Angela Browne (1985) developed a model of trauma that centers around possible long-term effects of victimization. These effects include feelings of powerlessness and shame, low self-esteem, a sense of betrayal, an inability to trust others, and the association of sex with trauma. This model may explain why some female crack cocaine users continue to return to settings in which they are verbally, physically, and sexually abused.

2. The physical environment included deteriorating and abandoned housing as well as substandard sidewalks and streets. The social environment reflected the replacement of a traditional community sense, the "Gemeinshaft" (Tönnies, translated by Loomis, 1957) by a "Gesellschaft," characterized by individualism, impersonal contacts, and distrust among community members.

Chapter Eight

1. Other researchers also confirm that people's memories often are impacted by current circumstances (Maines, Sugrue, and Katovich, 1983).

2. For a more in-depth discussion, see John Kaplan, *The Hardest Drug: Heroin and Public Policy* (Chicago: University of Chicago Press, 1983), and Ethan Nadelmann, "Drug Prohibition in the United States: Costs, Consequences, and Alternatives" in *Science* 245 (1989): 939–47.

Bibliography

Abramovitz, Mimi. *Regulating the Lives of Women: Social Welfare Policy from Colonial Times to the Present.* Boston: South End Press, 1988.

Adler, Patricia A. *Wheeling and Dealing: An Ethnography of an Upper-Level Drug Dealing and Smuggling Community.* New York: Columbia University Press, 1985.

———. "Ethnography and Epidemiology: Building Bridges." In *Proceedings of the Community Epidemiology Working Group.* Rockville, Md.: National Institute on Drug Abuse, 1993.

Agar, Michael H. *Ripping and Running: A Formal Ethnography of Urban Heroin Addicts.* New York: Seminar Press, 1973.

Alexander, Pamela C. "The Differential Effects of Abuse Characteristics and Attachment in the Prediction of Long Term Sexual Abuse." *Journal of Interpersonal Violence* 8 (1993): 346–62.

Amaro, Hortensia. "Considerations for Prevention of HIV Infection among Hispanic Women." *Psychology of Women Quarterly* 12 (1988): 429–43.

———. "Love, Sex and Power: Considering Women's Realities in HIV Prevention." *American Psychologist* 50 (1995): 437–47.

Andersen, Margaret L. and Patricia Collins. *Race, Class, and Gender: An Anthology.* Belmont, Calif.: Wadsworth, 1992.

Anderson, Elijah. *Street Wise: Race, Class, and Change in an Urban Community.* Chicago: University of Chicago Press, 1990.

Atlanta Regional Commission. *The Atlanta Metropolitan Area: Major Trends.* Atlanta, Ga.: Atlanta Regional Commission, 1995.

Ball, John C., Harold Graff, and John Sheehan. "The Heroin Addict's View of Methadone Maintenance." *British Journal of Addiction* 69 (1974): 243–48.

Ball, John C., John W. Schaffer, and David N. Nurco. "The Day-to-Day Criminality of Heroin Addicts in Baltimore: A Study in the Continuity of Offense Rates." *Drug and Alcohol Dependence* 12 (1983): 119–42.

Becker, Howard S. "Becoming a Marijuana User." *American Journal of Sociology* 59 (1953): 235–42.

———. *Outsiders: Studies in the Sociology of Deviance.* New York: Free Press, 1963.

225

Belle, Deborah. *Lives in Stress: Women and Depression.* Beverly Hills, Calif.: Sage Publications, 1982.

Bennett, Elizabeth and Kathi Kemper. "Is Abuse during Childhood a Risk Factor for Developing Substance Abuse Problems as an Adult?" *Journal of Developmental and Behavioral Pediatrics* 15 (1993): 426–29.

Berenson, David. "Powerlessness—Liberating or Enslaving? Responding to the Feminist Critique of the Twelve Steps." In *Feminism and Addiction,* edited by Claudia Bepko. New York: Haworth Press, 1991.

Biernacki, Patrick. "Junkie Work, 'Hustles' and Social Status among Heroin Addicts." *Journal of Drug Issues* 9 (1979): 535–51.

———. *Pathways from Heroin Addiction: Recovery Without Treatment.* Philadelphia: Temple University Press, 1986.

Binion, Victoria J. "Sex Differences in Socialization and Family Dynamics of Female and Male Heroin Users." *Journal of Social Issues* 38 (1982): 43–57.

Blackwell, Judith S. "Drifting, Controlling, and Overcoming: Opiate Users Who Avoid Becoming Chronically Dependent." *Journal of Drug Issues* 13 (1983): 219–35.

Blakely, Mary K. *American Mom.* Chapel Hill: Algonquin Books, 1994.

Blumer, Herbert. *Symbolic Interactionism: Perspective and Method.* Englewood Cliffs, N.J.: Prentice Hall, 1969.

Bourdieu, Pierre. "La Domination Masculine." *Actes de la Reserche en Science Sociales* 84 (1990): 2–31.

Bourgois, Philippe I. *In Search of Respect: Selling Crack in El Barrio.* New York: Cambridge University Press, 1995.

Bourgois, Philippe I. and Eloise Dunlap. "Exorcizing Sex for Crack: An Ethnographic Perspective from Harlem." In *Crack Pipe as a Pimp: An Ethnographic Investigation of Sex-for-Crack Exchanges,* edited by Mitchell S. Ratner. New York: Lexington Books, 1993.

Boyd, Carol. "The Antecedents of Women's Crack Cocaine Abuse: Family Substance Abuse, Sexual Abuse, Depression and Illicit Drug Use." *Journal of Substance Abuse Treatment* 10 (1993): 433–38.

Boyle, Kathleen and M. Douglas Anglin. "To the Curb: Sex Bartering and Drug Use among Homeless Crack Users in Los Angeles." In *Crack Pipe as a Pimp: An Ethnographic Investigation of Sex-for-Crack Exchanges,* edited by Mitchell S. Ratner. New York: Lexington Books, 1993.

Bryan, James. "Apprenticeships in Prostitution." *Social Problems* 12 (1965): 287–97.

Campbell, Carole. "Women and AIDS." *Social Science and Medicine* 30 (1990): 407–15.

Chasnoff, Ira J. *Drug Use in Pregnancy: Mother and Child.* Lancaster, Mass.: MTP Press, 1986.

————. "Cocaine, Pregnancy and the Neonate." *Women and Health* 15 (1989): 23–25.

Chavkin, Wendy. "Drug Addiction and Pregnancy: Policy Crossroads." *American Journal of Public Health* 80 (1990): 483–7.

Chiasson, Mary A., Rand Stoneburner, Deborah Hildebrandt, William Ewing, Edward Telsak, and Harold Jaffe. "Heterosexual Transmission of HIV-1 Associated with the Use of Smokable Freebase Cocaine." *AIDS* 5 (1991): 1121–26.

Coates, Thomas, Ron Stall, and Susan Kegeles. "AIDS Antibody Testing: Will it Stop the Epidemic? Will it Help People Infected with HIV?" *American Psychologist* 43 (1988): 859–64.

Cohen, Bernard. *Deviant Street Networks: Prostitution in New York City.* Lexington, Mass.: Lexington Books, 1980.

Cohen, Peter A. *Cocaine Use in Amsterdam in Non-Deviant Subcultures.* Amsterdam: Universiteit van Amsterdam, Instituut voor Sociale Geografie, 1989.

Collins, James and Margaret Allison. "Legal Coercion and Retention in Drug Abuse Treatment." *Hospital and Community Psychiatry* 34 (1983): 1145–49.

Collins, Patricia. *Black Feminist Thought: Knowledge, Consciousness, and the Politics of Empowerment.* New York: Routledge, 1991.

Cooley, Charles H. *Social Organization: A Study of the Larger Mind.* New York: C. Scribner's Sons, 1909.

Coombs, Robert H. "Drug Abuse as a Career." *Journal of Drug Issues* 11 (1981): 369–87.

Coombs, Robert H., Lincoln J. Fry, and Patricia G. Lewis. *Socialization in Drug Abuse.* Cambridge, Mass.: Schenkman, 1976.

Corea, Gena. *The Invisible Epidemic: The Story of Women and AIDS.* New York: Harper Collins, 1992.

Deitz, Sheila, Karen Blackwell, Paul Daley, and Brenda Bentley. "Measurement of Empathy toward Rape Victims and Rapists." *Journal of Personality and Social Psychology* 43 (1982): 372–84.

DeLaRosa, Mario, Elizabeth Lambert, and Bernard Gropper. *Drugs and Violence: Causes, Correlations, and Consequences.* Rockville, Md.: National Institute on Drug Abuse, 1990.

Deren, Sherry. "Children of Substance Abusers: A Review of the Literature." *Journal of Substance Abuse Treatment* 3 (1986): 77–94.

Deren, Sherry, Stephanie Tortu, and Rees Davis. "An AIDS Risk Reduction Project with Inner-City Women." In *Women and AIDS: Psychological Perspectives,* edited by Corinne Squire. London: Sage, 1993.

Dixon, Penelope. *Mothers and Mothering: An Annotated Feminist Bibliography.* New York: Garland, 1991.

Doll, Lynda, Paul O'Malley, Alan Pershing, and William Darrow. "High-Risk Sexual Behavior and Knowledge of HIV Antibody Status in the San Francisco Clinic Cohort." *Health Psychology* 9 (1990): 253–65.

Dunlap, Eloise and Bruce Johnson. "Family and Human Resources in the Development of a Female Crack-Seller Career: Case Study of a Hidden Population." *Journal of Drug Issues* 26 (1996): 175–98.

Dunlap, Eloise, Bruce Johnson, and Ali Manwar. "A Successful Female Crack Dealer: Case Study of a Deviant Career." *Deviant Behavior* 15 (1994): 1–25.

Ebaugh, Helen R. *Becoming an Ex: The Process of Role Exit.* Chicago: University of Chicago Press, 1988.

Edelman, Marian W. *Construction of the Political Spectacle.* Chicago: University of Chicago Press, 1988.

Ettore, Elizabeth M. *Women and Substance Use.* New Brunswick, N.J.: Rutgers University Press, 1992.

Fagan, Jeffrey. "Women and Drugs Revisited: Female Participation in the Cocaine Economy." *Journal of Drug Issues* 24 (1994): 179–225.

Farmer, Paul E., Margaret Connors, and Janie Simmons. *Women, Poverty, and AIDS: Sex, Drugs, and Structural Violence.* Monroe, Maine: Common Courage Press, 1996.

Faupel, Charles E. *Shooting Dope: Career Patterns of Hard-Core Heroin Users.* Gainesville: University of Florida Press, 1991.

Fields, Allen. "'Slinging Weed': The Social Organization of Streetcorner Marijuana Sales." *Urban Life* 13 (1984): 247–70.

Finkelhor, David and Angela Browne. "The Traumatic Impact of Child Sexual Abuse." *Journal of Orthopsychiatry* 55 (1985): 530–41.

Flaskerud, Jacqueline and Cecilia Rush. "AIDS and Traditional Health Beliefs and Practices of Black Women." *Nursing Research* 38 (1989): 210–15.

Fullilove, Mindy, Robert Fullilove, Robert Haynes, and Shirley Gross. "Black Women and AIDS Prevention: A View towards Understanding the Gender Rules." *Journal of Sex Research* 27 (1990): 47–64.

Gandossy, Robert P., Jay R. Williams, Jo Cohen, and Henrick J. Harwood. *Drugs and Crime: A Survey and Analysis of the Literature.* Washington, D.C.: Government Printing Office, 1980.

Garey, Anita. "Constructing Motherhood on the Night Shift: 'Working Mothers' and 'Stay-at-Home Moms.'" *Qualitative Sociology* 18 (1995): 415–37.

Gibbs, Jewelle. "Developing Intervention Models for Black Families: Linking Theory and Research." In *Black Families: Interdisciplinary Perspectives,* edited by Harold Cheatham and James Stewart. New Brunswick, N.J.: Transaction Publishers, 1990.

Giddings, Paula. *When and Where I Enter: The Impact of Black Women on Race and Sex in America.* New York: Bantam Books, 1984.

Goffman, Erving L. *Stigma: Notes on the Management of Spoiled Identity.* Englewood Cliffs, N.J.: Prentice Hall, 1963.

Goldstein, Paul J. *Prostitution and Drugs.* Lexington, Mass.: Lexington Books, 1979.

———. "Getting Over: Economic Alternatives to Predatory Crime among Street Drug Users." In *The Drug-Crime Connection,* edited by James A. Inciardi. Beverly Hills, Calif.: Sage Publications, 1981.

———. "The Drug/Violence Nexus: A Tripartite Conceptual Framework." *Journal of Drug Issues* 15 (1985): 493–506.

Goode, Erich. *The Marijuana Smokers.* New York: Basic Books, 1970.

Harrison, Diane, Karen Wambach, Joseph Byers, and Allen Imershein. "AIDS Knowledge and Role Behaviors Among Culturally Diverse Women." *AIDS Education and Prevention* 3 (1991): 79–89.

Hays, Sharon. *The Cultural Contradictions of Motherhood.* New Haven.: Yale University Press, 1996.

Heiss, Jerold. "Social Roles." In *Social Psychology: Sociological Perspectives,* edited by Morris Rosenberg and Ralph V. Turner. New Brunswick, N.J.: Transaction Publishers, 1981.

Herzberger, Sharon and Howard Tennen. "The Effect of Self-Relevance on Moderate and Severe Disciplinary Encounters." *Journal of Marriage and the Family* 47 (1985): 311–18.

Hewitt, John. *Self and Society,* 3d ed. Boston: Allyn and Bacon, 1984.

hooks, bell. *Ain't I a Woman: Black Women and Feminism.* Boston: South End Press, 1981.

———. *Yearning: Race, Gender, and Cultural Politics.* Boston: South End Press, 1991.

Hubbard, Robert L., Mary Marsden, J. Valley Rachel, Henrick J. Harwood, Elizabeth Cavanaugh, and Harold M. Ginzburg. *Drug Abuse Treatment: A National Study of Effectiveness.* Chapel Hill: University of North Carolina Press, 1989.

Hughes, Everett C. "Dilemmas and Contradictions of Status." *American Journal of Sociology* 50 (1945): 353–59.

Hughes, Patrick M. *Behind the Wall of Respect: Community Experiments in Heroin Addiction Control.* Chicago: University of Chicago Press, 1977.

Inciardi, James A., Dorothy Lockwood, and Anne E. Pottieger. *Women and Crack Cocaine.* New York: MacMillan, 1993.

Jaffe, Jerome H. "Footnotes in the Evolution of the American National Response: Some Little Known Aspects of the First American Strategy for Drug Abuse and Drug Traffick Prevention." *British Journal of Addiction* 82 (1987): 587- 600.

James, Jennifer J. "Prostitution and Addiction: An Interdisciplinary Approach." *Addictive Disease: An International Journal* 2 (1976): 601–18.

Johnson, Bruce D., Paul Goldstein, Edward Preble, James Schmeidler, Doug Lipton, Barry Spunt, and Thomas Miller. *Taking Care of Business: The Economics of Crime by Heroin Users.* Lexington, Mass.: D.C. Heath, 1985.

Johnson, Anne and Marie Laga. "Heterosexual Transmission of AIDS." *AIDS* 2 (1988): 49–56.

Kandel, Denise B. "Reaching the Hard-to-Reach: Illicit Drug Use among High School Absentees." *Addictive Disease* 1 (1975): 465–80.

Kane, Stephanie. "HIV, Heroin, and Heterosexual Relations." *Social Science and Medicine* 32 (1991): 1037–50.

Kaplan, Charles D., Bert Bieleman, and Warren TenHouten. "Are There 'Casual Users' of Cocaine?" In *Cocaine: Scientific and Social Dimensions* (Conference Proceedings). Groningen/Rotterdam: CIBA Foundation Symposium, 1992.

Kaplan, John. *The Hardest Drug: Heroin and Public Policy.* Chicago: University of Chicago Press, 1983.

Kearney, Margaret, Sheigla Murphy, and Marsha Rosenbaum. "Mothering on Crack Cocaine: A Grounded Theory Analysis." *Social Science and Medicine* 38 (1994): 351–61.

Kline, Anne, Emily Kline, and Emily Oken. "Minority Women and Sexual Choice in the Age of AIDS." *Social Science and Medicine* 34 (1992): 447–57.

Lazarsfeld, Paul F. and Robert K. Merton. "Friendship as Social Process: A Substantive and Methodological Analysis." In *Freedom and Control in Modern Society,* edited by Alan Berger, Theodore Abel, and Charles Page. New York: Octagon Books, 1954.

LeJeune, Chad and Victoria Folette. "Taking Responsibility: Sex Differences in Reporting Dating Violence." *Journal of Interpersonal Violence* 9 (1994): 133–40.

Lemert, Edwin M. *Social Pathology.* New York: McGraw-Hill, 1951.

Lewis, Sasha G. *Sunday's Women: A Report on Lesbian Life Today.* Boston: Beacon Press, 1979.

Lieb, John and Claire Sterk-Elifson. "Crack in the Cradle: Reproductive Decision Making among Crack Cocaine Users." *Journal of Contemporary Drug Problems* 12 (1995): 687–706.

Lofland, John. *Deviance and Identity.* Englewood Cliffs, N.J.: Prentice Hall, 1969.

Macdonald, Patrick, Dan Waldorf, Craig Reinarman, and Sheigla Murphy. "Heavy Cocaine Use and Sexual Behavior." *Journal of Drug Issues* 18 (1988): 437–55.

Maher, Lisa. "Criminalizing Pregnancy: The Downside of a Kinder Gentler Nation." *Criminal Justice* 17 (1990): 111–35.

Maher, Lisa and Richard Curtis. "Women on the Edge of Crime: Crack Cocaine and the Changing Contexts of Street-Level Sex Work in New York City." *Crime, Law, and Social Change* 18 (1992): 221–58.

Maines, David R., Noreen Sugrue, and Michael Katovich. "The Sociological Import of G. H. Mead's Theory of the Past." *American Sociological Review* 48 (1983): 161–73.

Marsh, Jeanne. "Public Issues and Private Problems: Women and Drug Use." *Journal of Social Issues* 32 (1982): 153–65.

Mays, Vickie. "AIDS Prevention in Black Populations: Prevention of a Safer Kind." In *Primary Prevention of AIDS: Psychological Approaches*, edited by Vickie Mays, George Albee, and Stanley Schneider. Newbury Park, Calif.: Sage Publications, 1989.

Melton, John. "The Relationship of an Alcoholic Family of Origin to Family Functioning and Quality of Life for Adult Children of Alcoholics." *Dissertations Abstracts* 53 (1993): 3689.

Miller, Eleanor M. *Street Woman*. Philadelphia: Temple University Press, 1986.

Minkhoff, Howard L., Jack A. DeHovitz, and Ann Duerr. *HIV Infection In Women*. New York: Raven Press, 1995.

Minkler, Meredith and Kathleen M. Roe. *Grandmothers as Caregivers: Raising Children of the Crack Cocaine Epidemic*. Newbury Park, Calif.: Sage Publications, 1993.

Mullings, Leith. *On Our Own Terms: Race, Class, and Gender in the Lives of African American Women*. New York: Routledge, 1997.

Musto, David F. *The American Disease: Origins of Narcotic Control*. New Haven: Yale University Press, 1973.

Nadelmann, Ethan. "Drug Prohibition in the United States: Costs, Consequences, and Alternatives." *Science* 245 (1989): 939-47.

Newcomb, Michael, Ebrahim Maddahian, and Peter Bentler. "Risk Factors for Drug Use among Adolescents: Concurrent and Longitudinal Analyses." *American Journal of Public Health* 76 (1986): 625–30.

Novello, Antonia. "Introduction." In *HIV Infection in Women*, edited by Howard L. Minkhoff, Jack A. DeHovitz, and Ann Duerr. New York: Raven Press, 1995.

Oakley, Ann. *Social Support and Motherhood: The Natural History of a Research Project*. Cambridge, Mass.: Blackwell, 1992.

Odets, Walt. "The Secret Epidemic." *OUT/LOOK*, Fall 1991.

Padian, Nancy, Stephen Shiboski, and Nicholas Jewell. "The Effect of Number of Exposures on the Risk of Heterosexual HIV Transmission." *Journal of Infectious Diseases* 161 (1990): 883–87.

Paone, Denise and Wendy Chavkin. "From the Private Domain to the Public Health Forum: Sexual Abuse, Women, and Risk for HIV Infection." *SEICUS Report* (1993): 13–16.

Pape, Patricia. "Issues in the Assessment of and Intervention with Alcohol and Drug Abusing Women. In *Clinical Work with Substance Abusing Clients*, edited by Shulamith Straussner. New York: Guilford Press, 1993.

Perkins, Roberta and Garry Bennett. *Being A Prostitute: Prostitute Women and Prostitute Men*. Sydney, Australia: George Allen & Unwin, 1985.

Powell, Douglas. "A Pilot Study of Occasional Heroin Users." *Archives of General Psychiatry* 28 (1973): 586–94.

Prins, Erick. *Maturing Out: An Empirical Study of Personal Histories and Processes in Hard-Drug Addiction*. Assen, Netherlands: van Gorcum, 1995.

Ratner, Mitchell S. *Crack Pipe as a Pimp: An Ethnographic Investigation of Sex-for-Crack Exchanges*. New York: Lexington Books, 1993.

Reinarman, Craig. "Constraint, Autonomy, and State Policy: Notes toward a Theory of Controls on Consciousness Alteration." *Journal of Drug Issues* 13 (1983): 9–30.

Roberts, Dorothy. "Punishing Drug Addicts Who Have Babies: Women of Color, Equality, and the Right of Privacy." *Harvard Law Review* 194 (1991): 1419–82.

Rosenbaum, Marsha. *Women on Heroin*. New Brunswick, N.J.: Rutgers University Press, 1981.

Rubin, Lillian B. *Worlds of Pain: Life In the Working-Class Family*. New York: Basic Books, 1976.

Schulenberg, John, Jerald Bachman, Patrick O'Malley, and Lloyd Johnston. "High School Educational Success and Subsequent Substance Use: A Panel Analysis Following Adolescents into Young Adulthood." *Journal of Health and Social Behavior* 35 (1994): 45–62.

Schur, Edwin H. *Labeling Deviant Behavior: Its Sociological Implications*. New York: Harper & Row, 1971.

Scott, James. *Weapons of the Weak: Everyday Forms of Peasant Resistance*. New Haven: Yale University Press, 1985.

Sidel, Ruth. *Women and Children Last: The Plight of Poor Women in Affluent America*. New York: Viking, 1986.

Silvia, Elizabeth B., ed. *Good Enough Mothering: Feminist Perspectives on Lone Motherhood*. New York: Routledge, 1995.

Singer, Merrill C. "AIDS and the Health Crisis of the U.S. Urban Poor: The Perspective of Critical Medical Anthropology." *Social Science and Medicine* 39 (1994): 931–948.

Skoll, Geoffrey R. *Walk the Walk and Talk the Talk: An Ethnography of a Drug Abuse Treatment Facility*. Philadelphia: Temple University Press, 1992.

Sobo, Elisa J. *Choosing Unsafe Sex: AIDS-Risk Denial Among Disadvantaged Women*. Philadelphia: University of Pennsylvania Press, 1995.

Spain, Daphne and Suzanne M. Bianchi. *Balancing Act: Motherhood, Marriage, and Employment among American Women*. New York: Russell Sage Foundation, 1996.

Stack, Carol B. *All Our Kin: Strategies for Survival in a Black Community*. New York: Harper and Row, 1974.

Staples, Robert. *The Black Woman in America: Sex, Marriage and the Family*. Chicago: Nelson Hall, 1973.

Stephens, Richard C. *The Street Addict Role: A Theory of Heroin Addiction*. Albany, N.Y.: State University of New York Press, 1991.

Sterk, Claire E. "Cocaine and HIV Seropositivity." *The Lancet* 1 (1988): 1052–53.

———. *Living the Life: Prostitutes and Their Health*. Rotterdam: Erasmus University Press, 1990.

Sterk-Elifson, Claire and Kirk W. Elifson. "The Social Organization of Crack Cocaine Use: The Cycle In One Type of Base House." *Journal of Drug Issues* 23 (1993): 429–41.

Strauss, Murray. "Family Patterns and Child Abuse In a Nationally Representative Sample." Paper presented at the 2nd International Congress on Child Abuse and Neglect, Washington, D.C., 1978.

Stryker, Sheldon. "Symbolic Interactionism: Themes and Variations." In *Social Psychology: Sociological Perspectives*, edited by Morris Rosenberg and Ralph V. Turner. New Brunswick, N.J.: Transaction Publishers, 1992.

Taylor, Avril. *Women Drug Users: An Ethnography of a Female Injecting Community*. Oxford: Clarendon Press, 1993.

Tennant, Forest and Artin Sagherian. "Double-Blind Comparison of Amantadine and Bromocriptine for Ambulatory Withdrawal for Cocaine Dependence." *Archives of Internal Medicine* 147 (1987): 109–12.

Thurer, Shari. *The Myths of Motherhood: How Culture Reinvents the Good Mother*. Boston: Houghton Mifflin, 1994.

Tönnies, Ferdinand. *Community and Society*, translated and edited by Charles Loomis. East Lansing: Michigan State University Press, 1957.

Tucker, Belinda. "Social Support and Coping Applications for the Study of Female Drug Abuse." *Journal of Social Issues* 38 (1982): 117–39.

Turner, Ralph V. "Role Taking: Process vs. Conformity." In *Human Behavior*, edited by Arnold Rose. Boston: Houghton Mifflin, 1962.

U.S. Department of Health and Human Services, Substance Abuse and Mental Health Agency. *Household Survey on Drug Abuse: Main Findings 1994* (Advance Report 7). Rockville, Md.: National Institute On Drug Abuse, 1995.

Van der Kolk, Bessel and Rita Fisler. "Childhood Abuse and Neglect and

Loss of Self-Regulation." *Bulletin of Menninger Clinic* 58 (1994): 145–68.

Waldorf, Dan. *Careers In Dope.* Englewood Cliffs, N.J.: Prentice Hall, 1973.

Waldorf, Dan, Craig Reinarman, and Sheigla Murphy. *Cocaine Changes: The Experience of Using and Quitting.* Philadelphia: Temple University Press, 1991.

Ward, Martha C. "A Different Disease: HIV/AIDS and Health Care for Women in Poverty." *Culture, Medicine, and Psychiatry* 17 (1993): 298–301.

Williams, Terry M. *The Cocaine Kids: The Inside Story of a Teenage Drug Ring.* Reading, Mass.: Addison-Wesley, 1989.

———. *Crackhouse: Notes from the End of the Line.* Reading, Mass.: Addison-Wesley, 1992.

Wilson, William J. *The Truly Disadvantaged: The Inner City, the Underclass and Public Policy.* Chicago: University of Chicago Press, 1987.

Winick, Charles. "Maturing Out of Narcotic Addiction." *Bulletin on Narcotics* 14 (1962): 1–7.

Wiseman, Jacqueline P. *Stations of the Lost: The Treatment of Skid Row Alcoholics.* Englewood Cliffs, N.J.: Prentice Hall, 1970.

Worley, Pascale and Patricia Fleming. "AIDS in Women in the United States: Recent Trends." *Journal of the American Medical Association* 279 (1997): 911–16.

Worth, Dooley. "Sexual Decision-Making and AIDS: Why Condom Promotion Among Vulnerable Women is Likely to Fail." *Family Planning* 20 (1989): 297–307.

Wright, Deborah and Paul Heppner. "Examining the Well-Being of Nonclinical College Students: Is Knowledge of the Presence of Parental Alcoholism Useful?" *Journal of Counseling Psychology* 40 (1993): 324–34.

Zausner, Michael. *The Streets: A Factual Portrait of Six Prostitutes.* New York: St. Martin's Press, 1986.

Zierler, Sally, Lisa Feingold, and Deborah Laufer. "Adult Survivors of Childhood Sexual Abuse and Subsequent Risk of HIV Infection." *American Journal of Public Health* 81 (1991): 572–75.

Zinberg, Norman E. *Drug, Set and Setting: the Basis for Controlled Intoxicant Use.* New Haven: Yale University Press, 1984.

Index

235